Frommer's

Bali
day BY day™
1st Edition

by Lee Atkinson

WILEY

Wiley Publishing Australia Pty Ltd

Contents

16 Favourite Moments   1

1 Strategies for Seeing Bali   7

2 The Best Full-Day Tours   11
The Best in Three Days   12
The Best in One Week   16
The Best in Two Weeks   20

3 The Best Special-Interest Tours   25
Bali with Kids   26
Artistic Bali   30
Spiritual Bali   34
Romantic Bali   40
Spa Horizons   42
Foodie Fling   46

4 The Best Regional & Town Tours   49
Kuta & Legian   50
Seminyak   54
Bukit Peninsula   58
Sanur   64
Ubud   68
Bali High   72
Eastern Bali   74
Northern Bali   78
Central Denpasar   82

5 The Best Beaches   85
Beaches Best Bets   86
Bali Beaches A to Z   88

6 The Great Outdoors 91
Adventures on Land 92
Bali on Foot 94
Watersports 96

7 The Best Accommodation 99
Accommodation Best Bets 100
Bali Accommodation A to Z 105

8 The Best Dining 115
Dining Best Bets 116
Bali Dining A to Z 123

9 The Best Shopping 137
Shopping Best Bets 138
Bali Shopping A to Z 142

10 The Best Nightlife 151
Nightlife Best Bets 152
Bali Nightlife A to Z 156

The Savvy Traveller 161
Before You Go 162
Getting There 165
Getting Around 166
Fast Facts 168
Bali: A Brief History 172
Useful Phrases 174
Phone Numbers & Websites 177

Index 178

Published by:

John Wiley & Sons Australia, Ltd

42 McDougall Street, Milton Qld 4064
Office also in Melbourne

Copyright © 2011 John Wiley & Sons Australia, Ltd.

National Library of Australia Cataloguing-in-Publication entry

Author:	Atkinson, Lee.
Title:	Bali day by day / Lee Atkinson.
ISBN:	978-1-74246-860-0 (pbk.)
Series:	Frommer's day by day city guide
Notes:	Includes index.
Subjects:	Bali Island (Indonesia)—Guidebooks.
	Bali Island (Indonesia)—Description and travel
	Bali Island (Indonesia)—Maps, Tourist.
Dewey Number:	915.98604

Cartographer: Lohnes+Wright

Production by Wiley Indianapolis Composition Services

Wiley also publishes its books in a variety of electronic formats. Some content that appears in print may not be available in electronic formats.

Printed in China by Printplus Limited

10 9 8 7 6 5 4 3 2 1

A Note from the Editorial Director

Organising your time. That's what this guide is all about.

Other guides give you long lists of things to see and do and then expect you to fit the pieces together. The Day by Day guides are different. These guides tell you the best of everything, and then they show you how to see it *in the smartest, most time-efficient way.* Our authors have designed detailed itineraries organised by time, neighbourhood, or special interest. And each tour comes with a bulleted map that takes you from stop to stop.

Hoping to relax on a pristine beach, catch the perfect wave, or stumble across an ancient temple in the middle of the jungle? How about taking a stroll through terraced rice paddies or following a religious procession? Whatever your interest or schedule, the Day by Days give you the smartest routes to follow. Not only do we take you to the top attractions, hotels, and restaurants, but we also help you access those special moments that locals get to experience—those 'finds' that turn tourists into travellers. The Day by Days offer one complete guide for all your travel needs. The best hotels and restaurants for every budget, the greatest shopping values, the wildest nightlife—it's all here.

Why should you trust our judgment? Because our authors personally visit each place they write about. They're an independent lot who say what they think and would never include places they wouldn't recommend to their best friends. They're also open to suggestions from readers. If you'd like to contact them, please send your comments our way at feedback@frommers.com, and we'll pass them on.

Enjoy your Day by Day guide—the most helpful travel companion you can buy. And have the trip of a lifetime.

Warm regards,

Kelly Regan

Kelly Regan, Editorial Director
Frommer's Travel Guides

About the Author

Lee Atkinson is a freelance travel writer and guidebook author based in Australia. Her travel stories regularly appear in the travel sections of various newspapers and glossy travel magazines, both in Australia and internationally. She is the author of seven travel guide books, including *Frommer's Sydney Day by Day, Frommer's Sydney Free and Dirt Cheap*, and a contributor to *Frommer's Australia.*

Acknowledgements

Thank you to all the people in Bali who pointed me in the right direction, gave me a lift, shared their food, welcomed me into their homes and made me laugh, especially my friends at Taliwanga in Kuta.

Thanks also to Bill, who never complains when I go missing in Bali for weeks at a time.

An Additional Note

Please be advised that travel information is subject to change at any time—and this is especially true of prices. We therefore suggest that you write or call ahead for confirmation when making your travel plans. The authors, editors, and publisher cannot be held responsible for the experiences of readers while traveling. Your safety is important to us, however, so we encourage you to stay alert and be aware of your surroundings.

Star Ratings, Icons & Abbreviations

Every hotel, restaurant and attraction listing in this guide has been ranked for quality, value, service amenities, and special features using a **star-rating system.** Hotels, restaurants, attractions, shopping, and nightlife are rated on a scale of zero stars (recommended) to three stars (exceptional). In addition to the star-rating system, we also use a **kids icon** to point out the best bets for families. Within each tour, we recommend cafes, bars, or restaurants where you can take a break. Each of these stops appears in a shaded box marked with a coffee-cup-shaped bullet 🍵.

The following **abbreviations** are used for credit cards:

AE	American Express	DISC	Discover	V	Visa
DC	Diners Club	MC	MasterCard		

Travel Resources at Frommers.com

Frommer's travel resources don't end with this guide. Frommer's website, **www.frommers.com**, has travel information on more than 4000 destinations. We update features regularly, giving you access to the most current trip-planning information and the best airfare, lodging and car-rental bargains. You can also listen to podcasts, connect with other Frommers.com members through our active-reader forums, share your travel photos, read blogs from guidebook editors and fellow travellers, and much more.

A Note on Prices

In the Take a Break and Best Bets sections of this book, we have used a system of dollar signs to show a range of costs for one night in a hotel (the price of a double-occupancy room) or the cost of an entree at a restaurant. Use the following table to decipher the dollar signs:

Cost	Hotels	Restaurants
$	under $100	under $10
$$	$100–$200	$10–$20
$$$	$200–$300	$20–$30
$$$$	$300–$400	$30–$40
$$$$$	over $400	over $40

How to Contact Us

In researching this book, we discovered many wonderful places—hotels, restaurants, shops and more. We're sure you'll find others. Please tell us about them, so we can share the information with your fellow travellers in upcoming editions. If you were disappointed with a recommendation, we'd love to know that, too. Please write to:

Frommer's Bali Day by Day, 1st Edition

John Wiley & Sons • 42 McDougall Street • Milton Qld Australia 4064

16 Favourite
Moments

16 Favourite **Moments**

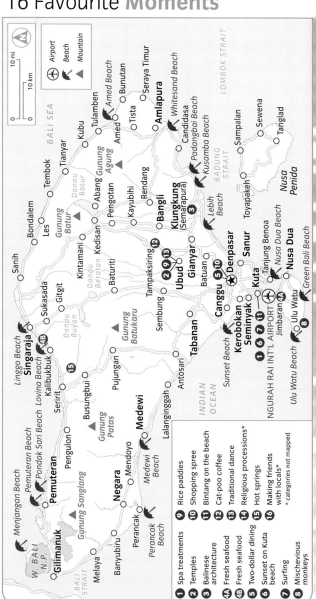

Airport
Beach
Mountain

Menjangan Beach
Linggo Beach
Pemuteran Beach
Pondok Sari Beach   Lovina Beach
Pemuteran
Singaraja
Kalibukbuk
Gunung Sanglang
Seririt
Gilimanuk
W. BALI N.P.
Sukasada
Gitgit
Banyubiru
Danau Buyan
Gunung Patas
Busungbiu
Pujungan
Gunung Batukaru
Antosari
Sembung
Tabanan
Lalanggingah
Medewi Beach
Medewi
Mendoyo
Negara
Perancak
Melaya
Perancak Beach
BALI STRAIT
INDIAN OCEAN
Canggu
Sunset Beach
Kerobokan
Seminyak
Kuta
NGURAH RAI INT'L AIRPORT
Jimbaran
Ulu Watu
Ulu Watu Beach

BALI SEA
Amed Beach
Bunutan
Seraya Timur
Tulamben
Amed
Tista
Kubu
Tembok
Tianyar
Abang   Gunung Agung
Whitesand Beach
Amlapura
Candidasa
Padangbai Beach
Bondalem
Les
Pengotan
Rendang
Kusamba Beach
Sanih
Kintamani
Kedisan
Kayubihi
Bangli
Klungkung (Semarapura)
Lebih Beach
BADUNG STRAIT
Danau Batur
Gunung Batur
Baturiti
Danau Beratan
Tampaksiring
Ubud
Gianyar
Batuan
Denpasar
Sanur
Tanjung Benoa
Nusa Dua Beach
Nusa Dua
Green Bali Beach
LOMBOK STRAIT
Sewena
Tanglad
Sampalan
Nusa Penida
Toyapakeh

1 Spa treatments
2 Temples
3 Balinese architecture
4A Fresh seafood
4B Fresh seafood
5 Two-dollar dining
6 Sunset on Kuta beach
7 Surfing
8 Mischievous monkeys
9 Rice paddies
10 Shopping spree
11 Bintang on the beach
12 Cat-poo coffee
13 Traditional dance
14 Religious processions*
15 Hot springs
16 Making friends with locals*

* categories not mapped

Previous page: Terraced rice paddies are a stunning feature of Bali's countryside.

There's nowhere else quite like Bali. At times chaotic and infuriating, it can also be serene and it's this unique mix of crass commercialism, intense beauty (both natural and man-made) and deeply entrenched spirituality that makes it such a magical place. From five-star luxury pool-villa retreats and sybaritic pampering to cheap-as-chips bargains on the beach, there's a Bali that suits everyone. Here are 16 special Balinese moments that make Bali such a special place for me.

1 **Being rubbed and pounded into a state of bliss for next to nix.** Spa treatments are ridiculously affordable in Bali, so there's no excuse not to have one every second day. Get your nails done, your hair conditioned, your feet nibbled by fish, your energy realigned, your body scrubbed and your muscles massaged—you might walk in, but you'll float out. *See p. 43.*

2 **Stumbling across a ruined temple in the middle of the jungle.** There's a temple on almost every corner in Bali, it seems. Some are overcrowded, over-commercialised tourist attractions, others are peaceful pockets of tranquillity amid the swirling chaos, but the ones I take most delight in are those you come across when you least expect to, smothered by jungle growth or crumbling away in the middle of a rice paddy. *See p. 35.*

Take advantage of the many cheap spa treatments Bali has to offer.

3 **Admiring the beauty of Balinese architecture.** From grand palaces to tiny temples, it's the little touches that make Balinese

An intricate architectural detail at the Museum Negri Propinsi Bali.

architecture so entrancing. A red hibiscus tucked behind the ear of a stone statue, an elaborately carved gate, a tiny courtyard pond covered in floating flowers, an elegantly curved roof line. In Bali, God really is in the details. *See p. 74, bullet ①.*

④ **Eating fresh seafood on the beach.** Watching the setting sun paint the sky red and gold through a haze of garlic-laden smoke wafting from grills loaded with hundreds of just-caught fish while the waves lap at your table legs on ④A Jimbaran Beach is one of those special only-in-Bali moments to cherish. The fish is just as good and just as fresh at ④B Lovina, but half the price. Even better, you'll only have to share your sunset view with a handful of others. *See p. 41 and p. 23.*

Bintang is the beer of choice.

⑤ **Dining out for \$2.** Roadside *warungs* (food stalls) and food carts offer superb Balinese food at incredibly cheap prices and some of the best meals I've ever eaten have cost me the equivalent of loose change. *See p. 60.*

⑥ **Sunset on Kuta Beach.** Whether you're lazing on a lounge at a fancy cocktail bar, sprawled on a plastic chair beside an esky full of beer at a beachside 'bar' on the sand or strolling hand-in-hand oblivious to the crowds, watching the sun sink into the sea on Kuta Beach is one of the greatest free shows around. *See p. 15.*

⑦ **Catching the perfect wave.** Doesn't matter if you're carving it up like Layne Beachley or a hopeless beginner like me, there's a perfect

Refreshment often comes on wheels in Bali.

These monkeys may look innocent, but they harbour criminal tendencies.

wave for everyone, whatever your surfing skills, in Bali. *See p. 97.*

8 Being pick-pocketed by a monkey. They might hang around in sacred forests and holy temples, but the mischievous monkeys of Bali are no angels when it comes to pinching food (and any other unsecured items) from your pockets or person. Despite their criminal tendencies you can't help but be captivated by their cuteness. I just wish I hadn't worn my best sunglasses last time I visited Ulu Watu. *See p. 70.*

9 Soaking in a view so green it hurts your eyes. Farming rice is more than just a way to make a living in Bali, it's an art form, and the terraced hillsides are a sight to behold. I love getting up early while the mist is still rising from the flooded rice paddies and watching the daily duck parade as it heads out to forage in the fields. *See p. 69, bullet 4.*

10 Getting a bargain. Knowing that you've paid half the price you would have for the same thing at home is a thrill. Finding something you could never find anywhere else is priceless. And paying more than you should for something you don't really want is all just part of the fun of a Balinese shopping spree. *See p. 144.*

11 Drinking an ice cold Bintang on a hot day. The beer tastes better in Bali. Maybe it's the heat, maybe it's the beach, and even though I never drink beer at home, there's nothing finer than nursing a cold Bintang at the end of a Bali day.

12 Sipping coffee made from cat poo. The insanely expensive coffee made from Kopi Luwak, the coffee beans that have been processed inside the gut of wild civets, is very good, but I have to confess that the real reason I love it so much is just because in Bali it's a tenth of the price you'd pay at home. *See p. 48, bullet 5.*

13 Being mesmerised by a fire and trance dance. There's no music, the chairs are made of plastic and if it's raining you'll get wet, but

Coffee made from Kopi Luwak is a tenth of the price you'd pay at home.

Religious processions featuring beautifully attired worshippers happen on a daily basis.

watching a Kecak performance in the darkened courtyard of a temple is an experience you're unlikely to forget as the men rhythmically chant themselves into a trance and dance with bare feet on hot coals. *See p. 157.*

⑭ Being held up by a religious procession. There's no denying that the endless traffic jams are one of the most infuriating aspects of travelling around Bali, but it doesn't seem to matter when you realise the hold-up is a parade of beautifully

Bathing in natural hot springs is a sure-fire way to dissolve any tension.

attired worshippers on their way to a temple or shrine carrying baskets of elegantly stacked fruit on their heads and roasted pigs hanging from bamboo poles balanced across their shoulders. I love that this happens on a daily basis and I love that nobody (except foreigners and expats) seems to mind the delay. *See p. 35.*

⑮ Soaking away your cares in a natural hot spring. Standing under a demon-head fountain that gushes a stream of thermally heated water onto your neck and shoulders is a sure-fire way to dissolve any tension. That the natural hot springs cost only a few cents to enter and are surrounded by lush tropical plants is a bonus. *See p. 81, bullet ⑪.*

⑯ Making friends with the locals. Whether your idea of a perfect holiday in Bali is a flop-and-drop break beside the pool, a week-long shopping expedition, a surfing safari or a cultural odyssey, one thing's for sure, wherever you stay, wherever you go, whatever you do, it will be the warmth of the Balinese that you'll remember most. ●

1 Strategies for Seeing **Bali**

Strategies for Seeing **Bali**

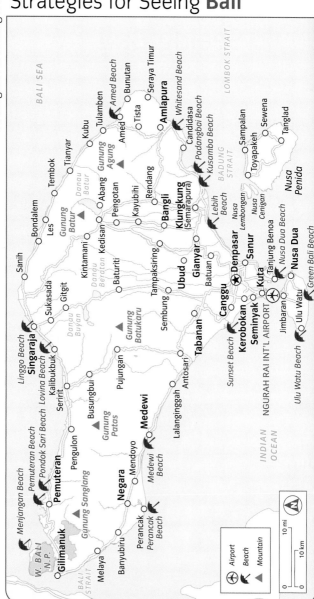

Previous page: Religious processions are one of the many colourful features of Bali.

Bali may be an island, but it's a big one. If you've only got a few days, don't try to see it all. Instead pick a base, either beside the sea or up in the hills, and do day trips from there. Exploring Bali is less about seeing the sights and more about getting to know the locals and gaining an insight into the local culture.

Rule #1: Be sun smart.
It can be tempting to spend your first day roasting in the sun as you warm those winter-chilled bones, but a dose of sunburn can not only make the rest of your holiday a painful affair (massages are not fun when you're burnt) it can also lead to skin cancer. Always wear plenty of sunscreen.

Rule #2: Slow down.
Bali's tropical heat and humidity can sap energy levels, so don't rush, and try and keep out of the sun in the middle of the day. Drink lots (water, not beer).

Rule #3: Don't drink the water.
While most of the ice served in restaurants and bars is made from purified water and is OK, tap water is definitely not. Always drink bottled or filtered water.

Rule #4: Relax, you're on holiday.
Don't try to do too much, or fit too much in. You're in Bali to wind down, so allow time to just chill out and do nothing. Massages work wonders when it comes to fast-tracking relaxation.

Rule #5: Patience is a virtue.
Things take longer to happen in Bali. You'll most likely learn this the hard way as you spend two hours in the immigration queue on arrival only to find yourself stuck in traffic on the way from the airport while a religious ceremony takes place in the middle of the road. Always allow plenty of extra time to get from A to B.

Rule #6: Take the time to chat.
Balinese people are friendly. Wherever you go, you'll be asked where you come from and where are you staying. They are not being nosy, or

Balinese people are friendly. Take the time to chat!

angling for a scam, it's just how Balinese work out who you are, and in 9 cases out of 10, it's a prelude to conversation.

Rule #7: Be polite.

Balinese people are also polite. Raising your voice or showing anger is considered extremely rude, so no matter how frustrated you are, keep it nice and you'll have more chance of getting things resolved the way you want.

Rule #8: Keep your cool.

The constant attention of people offering you transport or massages or trying to sell you something can be annoying and even infuriating. Don't lose your temper if they won't take no for an answer. Remember, they are only trying to earn a living. If you can't be polite, ignore them. They'll leave you alone once they realise they can't make a sale.

Rule #9: Bargain hard.

Practically everything is negotiable in Bali, including many items with a fixed price. Always ask for 'your best price', but don't get carried away trying to beat the seller down—in the end you're probably haggling over just a few cents. If you discover later that you paid way too much for something, chalk it up to karma—the seller's family will probably eat much better tonight thanks to you. *For bargaining tips, see* *p. 144.*

Rule #10: Get out and explore.

It can be very tempting to spend your entire holiday in Bali just lazing beside your hotel swimming pool (especially if you've got a pool villa), shopping or bar hopping. Bali has one of the richest cultures on the planet, and some of the most beautiful landscapes, so get out there and explore.

Rule #11: Forget about driving.

Sure, it's easy enough to hire a car, but the dearth of formal road rules and insane traffic makes driving in Bali an extreme sport. Hiring a car and driver is not only affordable, it's stress free.

Rule #12: Always carry a sarong.

Not only are they handy to dry off with if you find yourself with an unexpected swimming opportunity or soaked by a sudden downpour, but you'll need to wear one to enter a temple, whether you're male or female. *For more temple etiquette,* *see p. 39.* ●

Sarongs are an essential accessory.

The Best in Three Days

1	Pura Luhur Ulu Watu	
2	Jimbaran Fish Markets	
3	Jimbaran Beach	
4	Seafood Restaurants on Jimbaran Beach	
5	Goa Gajah	
6	Ubud	
6A	Neka Art Museum	
6B	Rice paddies	
7	Warung Ibu Oka	
8A	Jalan Wenara Wana (Monkey Forest Road)	
8B	Jalan Hanoman	
8C	Sacred Monkey Forest Sanctuary	
9	Kecak at Ubud Palace	
10	Kuta Beach	
11	Surf Schools	
12	Blue Ocean	
13	Shop Seminyak	
14	Sunset Cocktails at Ku De Ta	

Previous page: Pura Luhur Ulu Watu, one of Bali's most picturesque cliff-top temples.

On this three-day very-best-of-Bali tour we get a taste of everything that makes Bali so special—lots of sun, sand, surf, a stunning cliff-top temple, some art, a mesmerising fire trance dance and, of course, a bit of time for shopping. A beachside villa or hotel in Jimbaran is the perfect base. START: **Take a taxi to Ulu Watu on the Bukit Peninsula.**

Jimbaran beach is a perfect stretch of golden sand.

1 ★★★ Pura Luhur Ulu Watu.
Start your three-day whirlwind best-of-Bali tour with a moment or two of peace and quiet at one of Bali's most picturesque cliff-top temples. Early morning is the only time you'll escape the crowds, who flock here at sunset, and the cheeky monkeys will be too sleepy to make an effort to steal your sunglasses. Take a solitary walk along the coastline to the right of the temple for jaw-dropping ocean views. 🕐 *1 hr. See p. 35.*

2 ★★ Jimbaran fish markets.
No visit to Bali is complete without a visit to a local food market, and one of the most exciting is Jimbaran's fish market, where boatloads of still-twitching fish are haggled over at a fast and furious rate. 🕐 *30 min. See p. 59, bullet ❶.*

3 ★★★ Jimbaran Beach. From the market, stroll south down the beach until you find your perfect stretch of golden sand to laze away a few hours. Best swimming is at the very southern end, near the Four Seasons Resort, where the surf is also good for beginners. 🕐 *4 hr.*

4 ★★★ Seafood restaurants on Jimbaran Beach. One of the best things about basing yourself in Jimbaran, beside the glorious beach and laid-back vibe, is that one of Bali's very best experiences is right on your doorstep, a sunset dinner on the beach at one of the seafood warungs (food stalls) that Jimbaran is famous for. *See p. 60, bullet ☕5.*

You only have three days to see the best of Bali, so you've got a lot to cram in. Hire a car and driver for your second day, get up early and head to the hills, or more specifically Ubud, around an hour or so from Jimbaran.

5 ★★ Goa Gajah. Make your first stop the Elephant Cave, just east of Ubud. If you've arrived early enough, chances are you'll have the place to yourself and you can wander through the cave and surrounding jungle to a ruined temple in peace—without the busloads of gawping tourists it's very Lara Croft. 🕐 *1 hr. See p. 71, bullet ⓫.*

Picturesque terraced rice paddies surrounding Ubud.

6 ★★★ **Ubud.** Take a crash course in Balinese fine art at the **6A Neka Art Museum** (p. 31, bullet **1**) and trek back to the centre of town through the **6B rice paddies.** There's a track that leads off just near the Pura Dalem on Jl Raya Ubud, but if you're not sure, ask a local to point you in the right direction. ⏲ *2 hr.*

7 ★★★ **Warung Ibu Oka.** You'll have worked up an appetite by now, which is just as well, because one of the best eating experiences in Bali is not far away—

a paper cone full of the most succulent, melt-in-your-mouth, so-good-it-may-just-make-you-swoon suckling pig. *See p. 135.*

8 ★★ **Monkey Forest Road. 8A Jalan Wenara Wana** (also called Monkey Forest Rd), and parallel **8B Jalan Hanoman,** are Ubud's two main shopping streets. Jewellery, handicrafts and artist's studios are the main order of the day, although there are plenty of fashion boutiques as well. For those not interested in shopping, there are countless cafes. At the bottom of the hill both streets converge at the **8C Sacred Monkey Forest Sanctuary.** ⏲ *2 hr. See p. 70, bullet* **8**.

9 ★★★ **Kecak at Ubud Palace.** Late in the afternoon you'll start to see ticket sellers congregate around the Ubud Palace area, selling tickets to a range of evening cultural shows. Seek out a Kecak (or more commonly known for tourists as 'Fire and Trance Dance') performance: there's usually one performed every night in one temple or another in Ubud. If you're in luck, it will be in the very atmospheric Pura Dalem (Temple of the

Kecak, or 'Fire and Trance Dance', is a show you won't quickly forget.

Seminyak is Bali's top shopping destination.

Dead), but wherever it's performed it will be a show you won't quickly forget. ⏱ *2 hr. See p. 157.*

Day three, catch a taxi to the main gates of Kuta Beach, at the end of Jl Pantai Kuta.

⑩ ★★★ Kuta Beach. You can't leave Bali without seeing its most famous beach. If you want to take part in all the frenetic action wait until late morning, but if you prefer a quiet stroll on an uncrowded and relatively hawker-free beach, go early, when the local girls are still laying out flower-filled offering baskets on the high-tide mark and the sarong sellers are yet to arrive. The further north you walk, the quieter things get, so keep going until you weary, negotiate a good price for a beach umbrella, or pick a seat in the shade at one of the beachside *warungs* or 'bars' (plastic chairs grouped around an esky of cold beer) and chill out for a while. ⏱ *2–3 hr.*

⑪ ★★★ Surf schools. Bali's surf is the stuff of legends, but you don't have to be an expert to have a go. If you've never surfed before, Kuta's a great place to learn, with a host of surf schools to choose from and very competitive prices. ⏱ *1 hr. See p. 27, bullet* ❸.

⑫ Blue Ocean. The Blue Ocean has been serving up good-value meals since 1969 and it's a great spot for a casual lunch, just a stone's throw from the sea. *Jl Arjuna (Jl Double Six).* ☎ *(0361) 747 2308.* $$

⑬ ★★ Shop Seminyak. Some people come to Bali for the beaches, but many just come to shop, and the best place to shop is Seminyak. You could spend days here trawling the designer boutiques and homewares stores (many do), but if you stay focused, you should still be able to do some serious credit card carnage in an afternoon. ⏱ *3 hr.*

⑭ ★★★ Sunset cocktails at Ku De Ta. Anywhere that fronts the beach in Seminyak or nearby Double Six is a great spot for sunset drinks, but if you're only in town for one night, make it Ku De Ta—just be sure you've got the right clothes as beachwear at night is not allowed. And be warned, time has a habit of flying at this place and sunset drinks can easily turn into an all-night affair. ⏱ *1–3 hr.*

Ku De Ta is a great spot for sunset drinks.

The Best in One Week

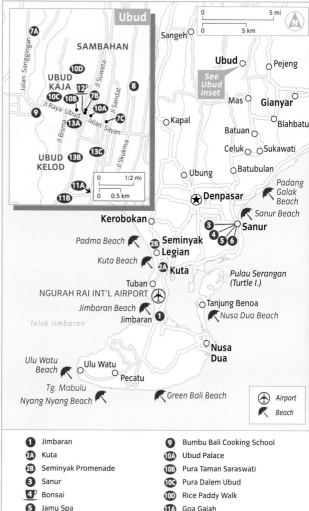

1	Jimbaran	**9**	Bumbu Bali Cooking School
2A	Kuta	**10A**	Ubud Palace
2B	Seminyak Promenade	**10B**	Pura Taman Saraswati
3	Sanur	**10C**	Pura Dalem Ubud
4	Bonsai	**10D**	Rice Paddy Walk
5	Jamu Spa	**11A**	Goa Gajah
6	Charming	**11B**	Sacred Monkey Forest Sanctuary
7A	Neka Art Museum	**12**	Warung Ibu Oka
7B	Blanco Renaissance Museum	**13A**	Jalan Raya Ubud
7C	Seniwati	**13B**	Jalan Wenara Wana
8	Botanic Garden	**13C**	Jalan Hanoman

A week in Bali means the best of both worlds. Spend half your time beside the sea, the other half immersing yourself in the rich Balinese culture to be found in and around Ubud. This week-long tour builds on our Best in Three Days tour, outlined previously in this chapter, with a day in Jimbaran and Seminyak using Jimbaran as a base, but also heads further afield to Sanur for an overnight stay before spending four days in Ubud. START: **Jimbaran on the Bukit Peninsula.**

1 ★★★ **Jimbaran.** For details on how to best spend your first day in Bali, see the early listings for 'The Best in Three Days' (p. 13). ⏱ 24 hr.

Catch a taxi to the main gates of Kuta Beach, at the end of Jl Pantai Kuta.

2 ★★★ **Kuta & Seminyak.** Day two is all about **2A** Kuta, more fun in the sun on the beach, an afternoon of retail therapy and a night of partying under the stars in **2B** Seminyak. You'll find detailed suggestions in 'The Best in Three Days' (p. 13). ⏱ 24 hr.

The easiest way to get from Jimbaran to Sanur is by taxi. It's about a 20-minute drive.

3 ★★★ **Sanur.** By now you'll need a change of pace after busy Seminyak and Kuta, and delightful Sanur is just the place for it. My favourite beachside location in Bali, Sanur has the perfect mix of laid-back shopping and wallet-friendly bars and restaurants, along with bucket loads of irresistible charm. Spend the morning strolling along the 4km **beachside promenade** (p. 65, bullet **3**) and visit the former home of Belgian artist Adrien Le Mayeur, now a charming, if a little ramshackle, museum, **Museum Le Mayeur** (p. 65, bullet **2**), before settling back at a beachside cafe for a long lunch. ⏱ 3 hr.

A fisherman on Jimbaran Beach.

The delightful beach at Sanur.

4 **Bonsai.** Grab a table on the sand and enjoy both the passing parade, fine beach views and some tasty Indonesian fare, although all the Western favourites are on offer as well. Don't forget to check out the bonsai garden before you leave. *Jl Danau Tamblingan 27.* ☎ *(0361) 282 909. $$*

5 ★★★ **Jamu Spa.** You've been in Bali for three days, so it's about time you had your first spa. Jamu's two-hour Ocean Detox, which includes a massage followed by a body scrub made from seaweed and sea salt crystals is just the ticket. ⏱ *2 hr. See p. 67, bullet* **12**.

6 **Charming.** You've indulged your body at Jamu, so now indulge your tastebuds with fine French fare in a charming open-air pavilion made from the reclaimed wood of old boats and local houses that lives up to the restaurant's name. *Jl Danau Tamblingan 97.* ☎ *(0361) 288 029. $$$*

It can be difficult to get a taxi to take you to Ubud without paying the return fare, and shuttle buses will take you on a circuitous route, so the best option if you don't want to waste precious time is to hire a car and driver for the one-hour trip.

7 ★★★ **Art and About in Ubud.** Ubud is the artistic heart of Bali, and you could spend three or four days just visiting the many art galleries and artist's studios in the area. With only three days at your disposal though, you'll just want to see the best, so head first to the **7A** **Neka Art Museum** (p. 31, bullet **1**) for an overview, then to the **7B** **Blanco Renaissance Museum** (p. 32, bullet **4**) in the flamboyant former home of the 'Dali of Bali', Spanish artist Antonio Blanco. Finish off your art odyssey at **7C** **Seniwati**, one of Bali's only museums dedicated to the art of women. ⏱ *3 hr. See p. 32, bullet* **7**.

Catch a ride on a motorbike taxi to the Botanic Garden, around 2km north of Ubud.

8 ★★★ **Botanic Garden.** Spend the afternoon admiring a different kind of art—the natural kind—at the Botanic Gardens. Highlights include the rainforest gully, bamboo grove, orchid garden and maze. The 20-minute walk back to town is a gentle, but utterly charming, downhill stroll

The Ubud Botanic Garden is enchanting.

walk. Check to see if there's a Kecak dance on here during your stay, it's spine-tinglingly atmospheric by firelight. ⏲ 6 hr. See p. 157.

Catch a taxi to Goa Gajah, 5km east of Ubud.

⑪ ★★ Jungle temples and Monkey Magic. On your last day in Ubud spend the morning in the jungle, firstly at the ⑪Ⓐ Goa Gajah (p. 71, bullet ⑪) and then fending off the too-cute residents trying to pick your pockets in the ⑪Ⓑ Sacred Monkey Forest Sanctuary (p. 70, bullet ⑨) ⏲ 3 hr.

Ubud Palace, in the heart of town.

through rice paddies. ⏲ 1–2 hr. See p. 70, bullet ⑦.

⑨ ★ Bumbu Bali Cooking School. Food, both the eating and cooking of it, is one of the cornerstones of Balinese culture, so where better to learn about Balinese cooking than in the cultural capital of Bali. The Bambu Bali cooking school includes a visit to the traditional produce market and a four-hour cooking lesson featuring six traditional Balinese dishes, but comes with a catch, you have to eat everything you cook at the end. Vegetarian classes are available. ⏲ 6 hr. Jl Suweta 1, Ubud. ☎ (0361) 974 217. Class costs 250000Rp per person. Bookings must be made one day in advance. Classes start at 9am.

⑩ ★★★ Palaces and Temples. The ⑩Ⓐ ★★ Ubud Palace (p. 69, bullet ⑤) is in the heart of town, so duck in and have a look and then spend the rest of the day visiting some of the many temples scattered around town. Two not to miss are the gorgeous ⑩Ⓑ Pura Taman Saraswati, with its lovely lotus pond and colourful statuary (p. 37, bullet ④), and jungly ⑩Ⓒ Pura Dalem Ubud (p. 37, bullet ⑤), the Temple of the Dead, where you can find the track that leads into the ⑩Ⓓ rice paddy

⑫ ★★★ Warung Ibu Oka. Don't squander your last opportunity to eat some of the best suckling pig in Bali at Warung Ibu Oka. See p. 48, bullet ⑥.

⑬ Retail therapy. This is also your last opportunity to shop, so take a stroll along ⑬Ⓐ Jalan Raya Ubud for antiques and art, down ⑬Ⓑ Jalan Wenara Wana (also called Monkey Forest Rd), for jewellery and handicrafts, and back up ⑬Ⓒ Jalan Hanoman for clothes and accessories. ⏲ 3 hr.

A resident of the Sacred Monkey Forest Sanctuary.

The Best in Two Weeks

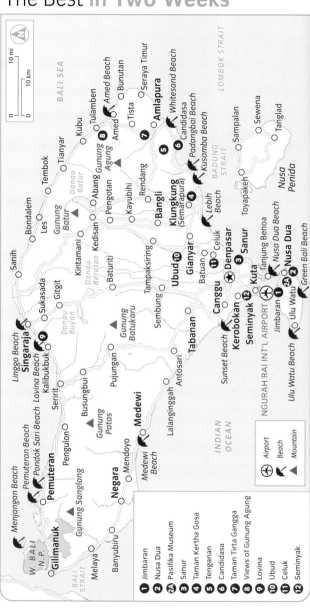

1 Jimbaran
2 Nusa Dua
2A Pasifika Museum
3 Sanur
4 Taman Kertha Gosa
5 Tenganan
6 Candidasa
7 Taman Tirta Gangga
8 Views of Gunung Agung
9 Lovina
10 Ubud
11 Celuk
12 Seminyak

Airport
Beach
Mountain

Get off the tourist trail and discover a different side to Bali in this two-week semi-circumnavigation of the island. Start with a night in Jimbaran and then kick back and relax for two days in the sun at Nusa Dua before making your way up the east coast via Sanur and Candidasa and along the undeveloped north coast to laid-back Lovina. Head back south over the mountains and take your time getting to know Ubud before hitting the golden sands and bright lights of Seminyak. START: **Jimbaran on the Bukit Peninsula.**

Travel tip

To really see the best of Bali on this tour you'll need your own transport. If you don't fancy braving the chaotic traffic on your own (and I don't blame you), you can use taxis for the short trips and hire a car and driver for the longer legs.

1 ★★★ **Jimbaran.** For details on how to best spend your first day in Bali see the early listings for 'The Best in Three Days' (p. 13). 🕐 24 hr.

Catch a taxi to Nusa Dua, around a 20-minute drive.

2 ★★ **Nusa Dua.** The beauty of having two weeks to spend in Bali is that you can afford to take time out and laze around the pool or on the beach for a day or two and Nusa Dua is the best place for it. Almost all the resorts are on the beach, have amazing pools, kids clubs and lots of resort activities, and there are properties to suit most budgets. If lying around all day becomes boring, there are plenty of action-packed **watersports** on offer (see p. 97), a 5km-long paved beachside pathway to walk or visit the excellent **2A Pasifika Museum** for a dose of high art (p. 61, bullet **9**). 🕐 2 days.

Catch a taxi to Sanur, around a 30-minute drive.

3 ★★★ **Sanur.** Spend your next two days in Sanur, which has a

beach every bit as good as Nusa Dua's, but there's more local life and colour to remind you that you're in Bali. 🕐 2 days. See 'Sanur' in chapter 4 (p. 65) for suggestions on what to see and do.

From here you'll either need your own vehicle for the next four days or hire a car and driver to take you to Candidasa via Semarapura. Total driving time is just over an hour, but allow extra time for traffic.

4 ★★ **Taman Kertha Gosa.** Bali's grand palaces are seldom that grand, but even though most of it was destroyed by the Dutch in 1908, what's left of the palace at Klungkung (Semarapura) is the

Sunset on Jimbaran Beach.

Sanur's colourful fishing boats.

exception that proves the rule. Spend some time wandering around the moated pavilions with their wonderful painted ceilings. ⏱ *1 hr. See p. 74, bullet* ❶.

❺ ★★★ **Tenganan.** This tiny village of Bali Aga people can seem a little touristy if you're unlucky enough to visit at the same time as a tour bus, but even so, it's still well

A guide pointing out the intricate details on the painted ceilings of Klungklung.

worth a visit, particularly if you're interested in traditional art and crafts, such as basket weaving, textiles, *lontar* (palm leaf) books or traditional musical instruments. ⏱ *1 hr. See p. 76, bullet* ❾.

❻ ★ **Candidasa.** While Candidasa (pronounced *Chan-di-da-sa*) may not have the glorious beaches of southern Bali, it has a certain charm that grows on you the longer you stay and makes an ideal overnight stop as you make your way up the east coast. It's pretty much at the end of the tourist trail, and those that are here tend to be of the more mature kind. There's no nightlife to speak of or shopping (do your shopping at Tengangan; see its review above), but there are some good restaurants and tourist tat is thin on the ground. ⏱ *Overnight.*

It's 114km from Candidasa to Lovina via the coast road, which should technically take around two hours, but allow half a day—chances are you'll be held up by a religious procession or two along the way.

7 ★★★ Taman Tirta Gangga.
Forget water slides and tiled swimming pools. The splendid water palace gardens of the last rajah of Karangasem, built in 1948, are the ultimate aquatic theme park and on a hot day there's no more opulent place to cool off, surrounded by ornamental ponds and multitiered fountains. ⏱ *1 hr. See p. 75, bullet 5.*

8 Views of Gunung Agung.
Once the road hits the north coast it can be difficult to know which way to look. On your left (if you have a fine day) are stunning views of Bali's highest and most scared mountain, the Gunung Agung volcano. On the right you are literally just metres away from the shoreline and it's one sweeping sea view after another. ⏱ *20–30 min.*

9 ★★★ Lovina. You're definitely off the tourist trail in Lovina. Hotels are cheap and simple and so is the food (think fresh fish grilled over an open fire on the beach, most likely by the fisherman who caught it), and while it does attract a few backpackers and divers, most of the

Prized roosters enjoy the sunshine near Ubud.

people who make it this far come here to do nothing. It's the perfect antidote to the teeming tourist hubs of southern Bali and the best place to actually meet and make friends with the locals beyond chatting up your friendly barman. Pull out a good book, find a shady spot and chill out. ⏱ *2 days. See 'Northern Bali' in chapter 4 (p. 79) for suggestions on what to see and do.*

The splendid water gardens of Taman Tirta Gangga.

It's around 90km to Ubud, up over the mountains, and a gorgeous drive. Allow 2½ hours. If you don't want to hire a car/driver, there are shuttle buses that depart from Lovina.

10 ★★★ Ubud. For many people Ubud, the cultural and artistic capital of Bali, is the highlight of their time here. Surrounded by beautiful rice paddies and jungle-clad hills, this collection of villages, now known collectively as Ubud, is home to hundreds of artists and artisans. Whether your interest is art, traditional music and dance, yoga and new age healing, hiking, white water rafting, Balinese cuisine or shopping, you'll find what you're looking for in Ubud. Although you could spend a week here easily, four days will give you plenty of time to explore the area and still sneak in some massage and relaxation time. ⏱ *4 days. See 'Ubud' in chapter 4 (p. 69) and 'Artistic Bali' in chapter 3 (p. 31) for suggestions on what to see and do.*

It's around 90 minutes driving time to Seminyak and southern Bali. There are plenty of shuttle buses that will get you there from Ubud, but hire a car and driver so you can stop at Celuk along the way.

11 Celuk. The silversmiths of Celuk have been banging out finely made jewellery for centuries, with skills handed down from father to son. The big commercial showrooms, where you'll get a hurried silver-making demonstration and then ushered into the shop for the hard sell, are on the main street, the smaller family-run ones, which are much more interesting, are in the backstreets. ⏱ *30 min.*

12 ★★★ Seminyak. By now you might be hankering for some non-Balinese food and sophisticated shopping, along with a little beach time. Seminyak has the goods, with plenty of European restaurants and high-end designer fashion. ⏱ *24 hr. For detailed suggestions, see 'Seminyak' in chapter 4 (p. 55).* ●

The sophisticated shopping of Seminyak.

Bali **with Kids**

- Penebel
- Melinggih
- Tampaksiring
- **8**
- **Bangli**
- Sembung
- Marga
- Sangeh
- Wanasari
- **Ubud**
- **7**
- Pejeng
- **Tabanan**
- Mengwi
- Mas
- **Gianyar**
- Kediri
- Kapal
- Batuan
- Blahbatu
- **4** Lebih Beach
- **6**
- Sukawati
- Singapadu
- Celuk
- Ketewel Beach
- Ubung
- Batubulan
- Padang Galak Beach
- **Canggu**
- **Denpasar**
- Sunset Beach
- **Kerobokan**
- Sanur Beach
- Padma Beach
- **Seminyak**
- **5**
- **Sanur**
- **Legian**
- Kuta Beach
- **Kuta**
- Pulau Serangan (Turtle I.)
- Tuban
- **1 2 3**
- NGURAH RAI INT'L AIRPORT
- Jimbaran Beach
- Tanjung Benoa
- Teluk Jimbaran
- Nusa Dua Beach
- Jimbaran
- **Nusa Dua**
- Ulu Watu
- Pecatu
- Nyang Nyang Beach
- Green Ball Beach

Airport
Beach

1 Waterbom
2 Braids on Kuta Beach
3 Learn to Surf in Kuta
4 Bali Safari & Marine Park
5 Flying Kites in Sanur
6 Bali Bird Park
7 Sacred Monkey Forest Sanctuary
8 Elephant Safari Park

0 — 5 mi
0 — 5 km

Previous page: A statue inside Pura Taman Saraswati, one of the most beautiful temples in Bali

B ali is a great place for kids. **Balinese love children** and are much more tolerant of cheekiness than we are. Don't be surprised if your kids get whisked away to be cuddled by friends and family in the kitchen while you're eating lunch. Nusa Dua is the best place for families, with hotels offering kids' clubs and a gentle beach that is great for paddling tots. And you're not far away from Bali's best kid-friendly attractions. START: **Tuban.**

1 ★★★ kids **Waterbom.** You don't have to be a kid to get a thrill out of this water-based theme park, although it helps. There's something for all ages, with 16 water slides and rides ranging from full-on adrenaline rushes to sedate floats, swimming pools, play areas, a swim-up bar, spa and restaurant. There's a special area for little kids under five and there are always lifeguards on duty. Kids will want to stay all day, but same-day re-entry is allowed if you want to ration the fun, and you can also buy two-day passes valid for a week. Children under 12 years old must be accompanied by an adult. ⏱ *2–4 hr. Jl Kartika Plaza, Tuban.* ☎ *(0361) 755 676. www.waterbom-bali.com. Admission US$26 adults, US$16 kids 2–12. AE, MC, V. Daily 9am–6pm.*

2 **Braids on Kuta Beach.** You're on holiday, so do something you'd never dream of doing at

home—give in to their pleas for a head full of braids. There's no shortage of women on Kuta Beach willing to relieve you of a few thousand rupiah to do the job. You might think your kids look silly, but they'll feel way too cool for school. Note: kids can get away with the look, adults just look ridiculous, so don't be tempted to join them. And since they'll be occupied, why not indulge yourself with a manicure and pedicure on the beach at the same time? ⏱ *15–30 min.*

3 ★★★ **Learn to Surf in Kuta.** Bali's a great place to learn to surf. There are a number of surf schools in Kuta and they cater for all abilities, although your kids will need to be good swimmers. Some schools have a minimum age of 12; others will accept younger kids but if they do, make sure they supply helmets. All provide soft boards and rash vests, and many will offer free

The kids will love Waterbom, with 16 water slides ranging from relaxing to hair-raising.

Kites are a fun, cheap and easy way to keep the kids entertained.

return transport from your hotel. All promise to have you standing up on your board by the end of your first lesson. Lessons vary in cost but are around US$30 to US$40 for a half-day lesson. We recommend **Quiksilver Surf School** (☎ (0361) 791 2220; www.quiksilversurfschoolbali.com) and **Pro Surf School** (☎ (0361) 744 1466; www.prosurfschool.com). ⏱ *2–3 hr.*

Sanur beach has lots of kid-friendly merchandise.

❹ ★ kids **Bali Safari & Marine Park.** Ride an elephant through the jungle, see white tigers, hippos on 'safari', meet orang-utans, get wet in the water park and watch a night-time cultural show with dancers and elephants. Half zoo, half theme park, it's a great day out for kids. A US$15 shuttle bus will take you to and from your hotel in Kuta, Sanur, Nusa Dua or Ubud. ⏱ *2–4 hr. Jl Bypass Professor Doktor Ida Bagus Mantra, Gianyar.* ☎ *(0361) 950 000. www.balisafarimarinepark.com. Admission US$12–45 adults and kids. AE, MC, V. Daily 9am–5pm, night shows at 6pm Tues & Sat.*

❺ **Flying kites in Sanur.** Just a few dollars will buy you a kite from any beachside seller or stall, but it will give you hours of fun. For real kite-flying action, head to Sanur during the annual Kite Festival in August. ⏱ *45 min. See p. 67.*

❻ ★ kids **Bali Bird Park.** It's not just the largest and finest collection of Indonesian birds in the world that captivates at this animal-based park just south of Ubud, but the range of exotic birds from the rest of the world and the Komodo dragon, crocodiles and snakes in the reptile park next door (included in the admission price). There's interactive feeding sessions, walk-through aviaries, free bird flight shows and a nursery with (mostly) cute little hatchlings. ⏱ *2 hr. Jl Serma Cok Ngurah Gambir, Singapadu, Batubulan.* ☎ *(0361) 299 352. www.bali-bird-park.com. Admission US$24 adults, US$12 kids 2–12. AE, MC, V. Daily 9am–5.30pm.*

⑦ ★★ kids Sacred Monkey Forest Sanctuary. Tiny tots not much taller than the monkeys may find their cheeky antics a little intimidating, particularly if you've got peanuts or bananas within reach, but most kids get a big kick out of the residents at Ubud's monkey forest. ⏱ *1 hr. See p. 70.*

⑧ ★★ kids Elephant Safari Park. Set up primarily as a refuge for abused and abandoned elephants that worked for loggers in the Sumatran forests, this place is a strange hybrid of conservation centre and elephant theme park. There are more than 30 pachyderms in residence and you can ride the elephants, watch the elephants paint, visit the elephant museum, see baby elephants or watch an elephant show. Still, even if they do have to spend their days doing tricks for tourists, I'm sure it's easier than hauling logs. There are some other rival elephant parks around, and drivers may want to take you there rather than this one because of higher commissions, so make sure you ask to be taken to the one at Taro and book direct with Bali Adventure Tours. It's around 15 to 20 minutes' drive north of Ubud. ⏱ *2–4 hr. Taro, 16km north of Ubud.* ☎ *(0361) 721 480. www. baliadventuretours.com. Combined safari park and ride tour US$86 adults, US$50 kids 2–12. AE, MC, V. Daily 8am–6pm.*

The Elephant Safari Park is a hybrid of conservation centre and elephant theme park.

Artistic Bali

Police Station

Post Office

1. Neka Art Museum
2. Sika Gallery
3. Art Zoo
4. Blanco Renaissance Museum
5. Museum Puri Lukisan
6. Rio Helmi
7. Seniwati
8. Agung Rai Museum of Art (ARMA)

U bud is the artistic heart and soul of Bali. It was here and in the surrounding villages that many foreign artists took up residence in the 1930s, with figures like Arie Smit inspiring and encouraging locals to paint, giving birth to the Young Artists Movement, and Walter Spies and Rudolf Bonnet, who formed the Pita Maha artists' cooperative to preserve the local fine art. Art lovers can spend days in and around Ubud visiting the museums, art galleries and small painter's studios, of which there are hundreds.
START: **Neka Art Museum, just west of Ubud.**

❶ ★★★ Neka Art Museum.
This is the best place to get an understanding of Balinese art. Each room has excellent explanations of the various art styles and each artwork has a detailed description of the subject matter, very handy when it comes to understanding the symbolism of the traditional works, which feature mythological tales and scenes from Hindu epics. This gallery has the best selection of contemporary Balinese art. There's also a large collection of work by Arie Smit, the Dutch painter who encouraged the young artists of the area to begin painting in the 1930s, and the country's largest collection of work by I Gusti Nyoman Lempad, Bali's most celebrated artist. Don't leave without seeing the gorgeous photographs of a vanished Bali taken by Robert A Koke between

1937 and 1941, when Kuta was just a fishing village, or the amazing collection of kris (ceremonial daggers). The gift shop has a good range of art books. ⏱ *90 min. Jl Raya Sanggingan.* ☎ *(0361) 975 074. Admission 40 000Rp. Daily 9am–5pm.*

❷ Sika Gallery. Pop into this little private gallery to check out what's happening on the contemporary art scene. Exhibits change every few months and always feature the work of a high-profile artist. ⏱ *10 min. Jl Raya Campuan.* ☎ *(0361) 975 084. Free admission. Daily 9am–5pm.*

❸ ★ Art Zoo. American artist Symon's working studio is a two-storey temple to bold, colourful and often irreverent art, strongly influenced by Warhol and the pop art movement. It makes a nice antidote

The Neka Art Museum is the best place to get an understanding of Balinese art.

to the reams of traditional and classical Balinese art you'll see in the big museums. ⏱ *15 min. Jl Raya Campuan.* ☎ *(0361) 974 721. www.symonstudios.com. Admission free. Daily 9am–6pm.*

④ ★★★ **Blanco Renaissance Museum.** The late Spanish artist Antonio Blanco was the self-styled Dali of Bali, and the theatrical artist's former home and studio have been transformed into a museum of his art set in whimsical gardens, complete with fountains, temples and an exotic bird collection. Imagine an Italian palazzo on Balinese acid and you'll get an idea of the style of his flamboyant and eccentric house, complete with stained-glass cupola in the ceiling. Climb up to the roof for good views of rice paddies and extravagant gold statues of Balinese dancers overlooking it all. The art itself, mainly portraits and dancers, is soft and serene. ⏱ *30–45 min. Jl Raya Campuan.* ☎ *(0361) 975 502. www.theworkstudios.com. Admission 50 000Rp (includes a welcome drink). Daily 9am–5pm.*

⑤ ★ **Museum Puri Lukisan.** The oldest fine arts museum in Ubud, it was established as part of the Pita Maha artists' cooperative founded by European artists Walter Spies and Rudolf Bonnet and with the help of prince Tjokorda Gede Agung Sukawati from the Royal Family in order to preserve and develop the blossoming art scene in Ubud in 1936. The focus is on modern and traditional Balinese art from the late 1930s through to the 1970s. The museum also runs a series of classes in everything from mask painting, kite making and wood carving to classical painting. Book at least one day ahead. ⏱ *30 min. Jl Raya Ubud.* ☎ *(0361) 971 159. Admission 40 000Rp. Daily 9am–5pm (closed on major Balinese holy days).*

⑥ ★ **Rio Helmi.** Be inspired by the large-format photographs of photo journalist Rio Helmi to get out there early in the morning and take your own shots. Some of the images displayed are from his assignments in Europe and throughout Southeast Asia, but his Balinese photographs of religious ceremonies and rituals are particularly evocative. Limited edition prints are for sale. ⏱ *15 min. Jl Suweta 24A.* ☎ *(0361) 978 773. Free admission. Daily noon–8pm.*

⑦ ★ **Seniwati.** You won't see much (if any) art by women hanging in the galleries and art museums of Ubud and Bali and Seniwati tries to fill that gap. This museum of art by women—from Bali, Indonesia and even some visiting foreign women artists, but all resident in Bali—is not big, just five small rooms, but it provides an interesting female view of Balinese life, and it's not nearly as rosy as that painted by men. Much of the work is also for sale. ⏱ *15 min. Jl Sriwedari 2B.* ☎ *(0361) 975 485. Free admission. Tues–Sun 9am–5pm.*

The stained glass cupola is just one feature of the eccentric building that houses the Blanco Renaissance Museum.

Lempad's Rice Harvest, at Museum Puri Lukisan.

8 ★★ **Agung Rai Museum of Art (ARMA).** This grand museum is the best place to see the work of German Artist Walter Spies, although sadly the paintings are all reproductions, but at least it will give you an idea of how influential his work was in Bali. The rest of the museum focuses on traditional and classical Balinese art, particularly of the Pita Maha artists' co-operative, and modern Balinese art. The sculpture-studded gardens are well worth a wander, and this is the best place to take an art course in painting, wood carving or batik. It's also a centre for the performing arts, and you'll often see school children learning classical dances here, which can be quite charming to watch. ⏱ *1 hr. Jl Raya Pengosekan.* ☎ *(0361) 976 659. Admission 40 000Rp. Daily 9am–6pm.*

Art Beyond Ubud

Three other art museums worth visiting are the State Museum (**Museum Negri Propinsi Bali**) in Denpasar, where one of the pavilions is dedicated to Balinese art and provides a brief overview of the various Balinese art movements, from ancient temple sculpture and paintings through to contemporary works (see p. 82). In Nusa Dua the **Pasifika Museum** not only has an extensive collection of Classical Balinese paintings, but also rooms of work by colonial Dutch painters, and visiting and resident Asian and Western artists. It's worth visiting for the Donald Friend room alone, and it even has work by luminaries such as Gauguin and Matisse (see p. 61). The **Museum Le Mayeur** in Sanur is a favourite. It's a bit shabby around the edges, but Adrien Le Mayeur's beachside Balinese house is full of the Belgian artist's dreamy paintings, mostly of his beautiful wife, dancer Ni Pollack (see p. 65).

Spiritual Bali

Gunung Penulisan ▲
Songan
Gunung Batur ▲
Kintamani ○ ❻ ○ Batur   Danau   Gunung
Kalanganyar ○   Batur   Abang ▲
            Kedisan ○   ○ Abang
Wanagiri ○
Danau
Tamblingan   Danau
            Beraten
Gunung   Pengotan ○
Lesung ▲
    Gunung
    Pohen ▲   Besakih ○ ❼
▲   ○ Baturiti   ○ Kayubihi
Gunung
Batukaru   Menanga ○   Muncan ○
○ Wongayagede   ○ Petang   Rendang ○   ○
                    ○ Melinggih
○ Penebel   ○ Bangli
            Tampaksiring ○   Sidemen ○
    Sembung ○   ○ Sangeh
    Marga ○   Klungkung
Wanasari ○   Ubud ○ ❹❺   (Semarapura)
Tabanan ○   Mengwi ○ ❸   ○ Pejeng   ○
Kediri ○   ○ Kapal   Mas ○   ○ Gianyar   Kusamba ○
                    Batuan ○   ○ Blahbatu
                    Celuk ○ ○ Sukawati   Lebih Beach ➤
❷   ○ Ubung   ○ Batubulan   Ketewel Beach ➤   BADUNG
Sunset ➤   ○ Canggu   ★ Denpasar   STRAIT
Beach   ➤ Padang Galak Beach
Kerobokan ○   ❽ Sanur   ➤ Sanur Beach
Padma Beach ➤   Seminyak   Jungutbatu ○
    Legian ○   Pulau Serangan   Nusa Lembongan
Kuta Beach ➤   ○ Kuta   (Turtle I.)
        Tuban ○   Nusa Ceningan
NGURAH RAI INT'L ✈   ○ Tanjung Benoa
Jimbaran Beach ➤
    Teluk   Jimbaran
    Jimbaran   ○   ➤ Nusa Dua Beach
Ulu Watu ○   Nusa Dua
❶   ○ Pecatu
Tg.
Mabulu ➤   ✈ Airport
Nyang   Green Bali ➤   ➤ Beach
Nyang   Beach
Beach   ▲ Mountain
                    ➤ Scuba Diving

❶ Pura Luhur Ulu Watu
❷ Tanah Lot
❸ Pura Taman Ayun
❹ Pura Taman Saraswati
❺ Pura Dalem Ubud
❻ Pura Batur
❼ Pura Besakih
❽ Pura Jagatnatha

Bali is an immensely spiritual place. It's impossible to walk along a street without passing hundreds of tiny palm-leaf baskets full of flowers and food for the gods left on footpaths and outside doorways, sometimes even in the middle of the road. Everywhere you go you'll see women making offerings and burning incense at tiny shrines. For the Balinese, this type of religious worship and ritual is a daily affair and the local temple is an integral part of everyday life. The temples are also the island's most elaborate and beautiful buildings, and some, like Tanah Lot, are Bali's most popular tourist attractions; others are islands of peace and quiet and offer a fleeting glimpse of Bali's beautiful soul. START: **Ulu Watu, around 30 minutes' drive east of Jimbaran.**

❶ ★★★ **Pura Luhur Ulu Watu.** There's been a temple perched precipitously on the cliff top at Ulu Watu since the 11th century. As a non-Hindu you can't enter the temple courtyard, but the reason to come here is for the amazing views of the line of sheer cliffs pounded by super-sized surf that this part of the southern coast is famous for. Best views are at the end of a short walk along the cliff edge and through the forest on the right-hand side, although the views on the left are pretty good too, and less crowded if it's busy. Like Bali's other famous sea temple Tanah Lot, Ulu Watu is a popular early evening spot when tour buses from Kuta and Nusa Dua arrive to take in the sunset and often a traditional Kecak dance in which the singers enter a trance as they chant. Go early in the morning and you'll have the place to yourself.

Unlike Tanah Lot, however, it's mercifully free of the hawkers and sarong sellers, although the resident monkeys can be an even more irritating menace. They're very cute to look at, until they pinch your sunglasses, handbag or cap and run off with them, so try to keep your belongings close. 🕐 *1 hr. Admission 3000Rp, parking fee (even if coming by taxi) 1000Rp, Kecak dance around 70 000Rp.*

From Ulu Watu head to Kutu and Seminyak and take the coast road west beyond Kerobokan and follow the signs. Allow at least 90 minutes to get to Tanah Lot from Ulu Watu (half an hour from Seminyak), depending on traffic.

❷ **Tanah Lot.** This small temple on a rock island west of Kuta is one of the most venerated by Balinese. As a non-Balinese you can't actually

Beautiful offerings are found everywhere in Bali.

Tanah Lot, one of the most venerated temples in Bali.

enter the temple, which is accessible only during low tide, so visiting here is all about taking in the rugged coastline views. But it's your classic catch 22; the best time to see it is at sunset, when the tiered *meru* (multi-roofed shrine or pagoda) is silhouetted against a red wine sky (which is not always guaranteed). But there's usually so many tourists that you'll be lucky to see anything at all beyond a crowd of heads. Go in the morning and you can get a better view, and even moments of solitude if you head up the hill to the row of terraced cafes that have a prime sunset-viewing position, although only half are actually open for business during the morning hours. This is the temple that's on all the postcards and one of the most popular

Religious processions are a very common sight.

day trips from South Bali, so treat it as a tourist attraction rather than a holy place. And be prepared to run the gamut of 'art' shops and DVD, Bintang T-shirt and sarong sellers, as well as the inevitable shopping strip of stores selling brands from home like Crocs and Polo, between the car park (which is bigger than the temple itself) and the temple gate. ⏲ *1 hr. Admission 10 000Rp.*

Head inland to Mengwi, 16km northwest of Denpasar.

❸ ★★★ Pura Taman Ayun.
This is how a temple should be, an oasis of calm and tranquillity. Despite being a stop on many tours to Tanah Lot, this former Royal Temple at Mengwi, built in 1634, is free of T-shirt sellers and the like and seems to swallow up the crowds the way other temples can't. Perhaps it's the beautiful gardens that surround the complex of three interconnecting yards. Most tours only stop here for half an hour, but if you can avoid the pre-sunset crush around 3pm to 4pm, you can wander almost alone on the riverside paths or relax in one of the many pavilions scattered around the grounds that are perfect for a moment or 20 of peaceful contemplation. ⏲ *1–2 hr. Admission 3000Rp.*

Continue northeast to Ubud, wiggling your way along back roads and through tiny villages such as Baha and Penarungan, hooking

Cremation Ceremony

Spend any time at all in Bali and chances are you'll come across a cremation ceremony or procession. Led by a black and gold bull that becomes the funeral pyre, the body is carried to the cremation ground in an ornate multilevel tower made of bamboo, paper, string, tinsel, silk, cloth, mirrors, flowers and anything else bright and colourful (the higher the tower, the richer the deceased). Unlike cremation ceremonies in the West, it's anything but sombre, with plenty of loud music, raucous horn blowing and cheerful cheering—a display of sadness is believed to prevent the soul's release from the body.

up with the main road to Ubud at Mas. Allow at least 40 minutes.

4 ★★ Pura Taman Saraswati. This small temple in the middle of busy Ubud is one of the most beautiful in Bali. Set beside a large lotus pond, once inside the gates it's a riot of colour, with lots of red and gold touches to the stone and wooden carvings everywhere. That it's dedicated to Dewi Saraswati, the goddess of wisdom and the arts, comes as no surprise given that Ubud is the artistic centre of Bali. There are cultural performances outside the main gate beside the pond every night, except Wednesdays and Fridays. ⏱ 15 min. Jl Raya Ubud. See p. 37.

5 ★★ Pura Dalem Ubud. One of my favourite temples in Ubud, the 'Temple of the Dead' features a huge Banyan tree in the middle of the main courtyard and has a wonderfully mysterious jungle feel to it, kind of fitting given it's devoted to death. This is where many cremations are carried out. Despite this dedication to the dark side, many of the gates and the pavilion are

Pura Taman Saraswati, a temple dedicated to Dewi Saraswati, goddess of wisdom and the arts.

Pura Besakih, Bali's spiritual heart.

lavishly decorated in red and gold leaf. 🕐 *15 min. Jl Raya Ubud.*

From Ubud follow the main road north and hook up with Jl Tirta Tawar to Danau Batur. Allow at least an hour.

6 Pura Batur. This temple, precariously perched on the rim of the volcano, is the second most important temple in Bali, outranked only by Besakih (below). The original temple was destroyed when Gunung Batur erupted in 1926. Dedicated to the Goddess of the Crater Lake, Pura Batur is believed to control the water for all the island's irrigation systems, so expect to see plenty of rice farmers making

offerings to protect their livelihoods. 🕐 *30 min. Admission 10 000Rp.*

Follow Jl Raya Penelokan and then Jl Besakih southeast. The main entrance to the temple is on the road from Menanga. Ignore the signs to the first car park and head to the second, northern parking area, which is 300m closer to the complex (signposted Kintamani, ignore the sign pointing right to Besakih unless you want to walk up the hill).

7 ★★ Pura Besakih. Known as the 'Mother Temple', this is Bali's spiritual heart, although as a visitor the commercialism that surrounds the temple can make it feel anything

A religious procession on the beach.

Temple Etiquette

When visiting a temple you should make sure your knees and shoulders are covered. Many temples, particularly the important or state temples, will provide a sarong and sash on entering in return for a small donation. The sash, called a *selandong*, is seen as a mark of respect. If watching a ceremony, do not put yourself in a higher position than the priest (this is often inadvertently done in the quest for the perfect photo). There are special rules for women: you may not enter a temple if menstruating, pregnant or have recently given birth, as women are considered to be ritually unclean during these times.

but. Try and ignore the touts and focus on the beautiful architecture in the extensive complex of 23 temples, including the *candi bentar* (split gateway). It's perched 1000m up on the slopes of Gunung Agung, Bali's highest volcano, and the view from the top of the temple over the myriad towers is quite impressive.

🕐 *90 min. Admission 10 000Rp. Guides are not compulsory but they'll try to convince you they are because 'the temple is closed today for an important ceremony'. If you do decide to take up their services, and they can be useful, the price is by 'donation'. Around 25 000Rp is a fair price per person, don't let them pressure you into paying more.*

Jl Besakih continues southeast to the coast south of Klungkung. From there, the main road (Jl Profesor Doktor Ida Bagus Mantra) will lead you straight into Denpasar. Pura Jagatnatha is opposite Puputan Square (Jl Gajah Mada). Allow 90 minutes.

8 Pura Jagatnatha. Pura Besakih may be the mother temple, but the official state temple is in the capital, Denpasar. Built in 1953, it differs from most other Balinese temples in that it is dedicated to one god rather than many, the supreme god, Sanghyang Widi. The complex consists of a coral shrine (originally white, but blackened by pollution) surrounded by a small moat and countless statues. It's a lovely place to escape the traffic and bustle of Denpasar, and gets very few tourists, so it doesn't feels like a tourist attraction the way many of the other big temples do.

🕐 *15 min. Jl Gajah Mada. Admission by donation.*

Pura Jagatnatha, the official state temple.

Romantic Bali

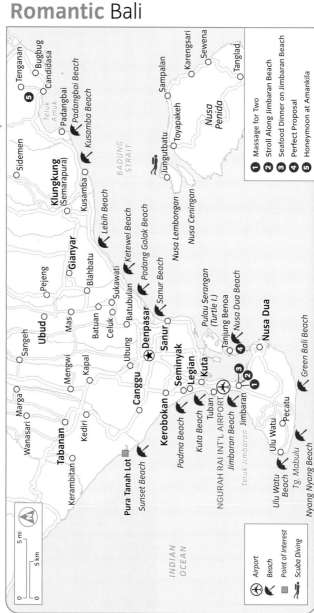

1 Massage for Two
2 Stroll Along Jimbaran Beach
3 Seafood Dinner on Jimbaran Beach
4 Perfect Proposal
5 Honeymoon at Amankila

Tenganan
Bugbug
Candidasa
Padangbai
Padangbai Beach
Kusamba Beach

Sidemen
Teluk Amuk
Sampalan
Karengsari
Sewena
Tanglad

Klungkung (Semarapura)
Kusamba
Lebih Beach
BADUNG STRAIT
Nusa Penida

Gianyar
Blahbatu
Ketewel Beach
Padang Galak Beach
Jungutbatu
Toyapakeh

Pejeng
Ubud
Mas
Batuan
Celuk
Sukawati
Batubulan
Ubung
Denpasar
Sanur
Sanur Beach
Nusa Lembongan
Nusa Ceningan

Sangeh
Mengwi
Kapal
Canggu
Seminyak
Legian
Kuta
Pulau Serangan (Turtle I.)
Tanjung Benoa
Nusa Dua Beach
Nusa Dua

Marga
Kerobokan
Padma Beach
Kuta Beach
Tuban
NGURAH RAI INT'L AIRPORT
Jimbaran Beach
Jimbaran
Green Bali Beach

Tabanan
Wanasari
Kediri
Pura Tanah Lot
Sunset Beach
Teluk Jimbaran
Ulu Watu
Pecatu

Kerambitan
Ulu Watu Beach
Tg. Mabullu
Nyang Nyang Beach

INDIAN OCEAN

5 mi
5 km
0

Airport
Beach
Point of Interest
Scuba Diving

B ali brings out the romantic in even the most pragmatic soul. Surrounded by art and beauty and beautiful views, how can you resist? Spend up big on luxe pool villas and ritzy massage treatments for two, or keep it cheap and cheerful at sunset on one of the world's most romantic beaches. Either way, you'll be seduced. START: **Jimbaran.**

① ★★★ **Massage for two.** Kick off your romantic holiday in Bali with a very Balinese treat, a couples massage. Guaranteed to get you relaxed and feeling good, there is no better way to spend time together. And in Bali, a couples massage is much more affordable than just about anywhere else. Most hotel and resort spas have treatment rooms designed for two, but a favourite is **Ayana's Spa on the Rocks at** Ayana Resort and Spa. *See p. 107.*

② ★★★ **Stroll along Jimbaran Beach.** A deserted beach can sometimes be hard to find in Bali, but the almost perfect stretch of white sand at Jimbaran has plenty of space for everyone to find a small patch of solitude. It's perfect for long romantic hand-in-hand strolls, with plenty of places to stop for a drink or snack along the way.

③ ★★★ **Seafood dinner on Jimbaran Beach.** While the sunset seafood dinners served up on Jimbaran Beach are certainly magical, it can be hard to be romantic when you are surrounded by

The Conrad Bali's beachside cabanas are a great spot for a romantic dinner.

A massage for two is the perfect way to kick off your romantic holiday.

thousands of fellow diners. For around a million rupiah (US$100 to $110), you get your own special table at the water's edge, a seafood feast for two with wine, flowers, silk umbrellas and private waiter. I recommend ★ **Teba Cafe**. *See p. 134.*

④ ★★★ **Perfect proposal.** Got something special you want to announce—or ask? A private candlelit beach bale festooned with floaty fabrics and bathed in moonlight is the perfect place. And if you do pop the question, you can always get married on-site: the **Conrad Bali** has its own seaside wedding chapel and will organise everything for you. *See p. 109.*

⑤ ★★★ **Honeymoon at Amankila.** Some private pool villas are like a self-contained resort for two—with everything you need so you never need to leave. My favourite is **Amankila**. *See p. 106.*

Spa Horizons

1. Massage on Kuta Beach
2. Kenko Reflexology
3. Jari Menari
4. Fish Spa
5. Jamu Spa School
6. Ubud Yoga Centre
7. Sound Massage
8. Meditation in the Rainforest
9. Ubud Sari Health Resort

Pampering and wellness in Bali is all about being pummelled and pounded into a deep state of bliss. Balinese massage is part of the traditional culture and almost every hotel, even the cheapies, will offer spa and massage treatments. In the south, there are literally thousands of places where you can be poked, prodded, massaged, manicured and soothed at prices to suit any budget (and that doesn't include the massage ladies on the beach). Things are bit more holistic in Ubud, where healing is just as important as feeling good. START: **Kuta Beach.**

❶ Massage on Kuta Beach.

I can guarantee that it will take less than 20 seconds before you are offered a massage on Kuta Beach. They last around 20 minutes, are more like a rub down with oil (with a bit of accidental sand mixed in for some serendipitous exfoliation) than a therapeutic pummelling and cost the equivalent of US$2 or US$3 (depending on your bargaining skills). They are definitely not the best massage experience you'll have in Bali, but they're a quintessential Bali experience nonetheless.

❷ ★★★ Kenko Reflexology. A

one-hour foot and full-body reflexology and pressure massage at this unassuming little place in Legian is definitely about wellness, rather than pampering. The massage is done in one of six reclining chairs

with no privacy screens, by an all-male masseur team, and you keep all your clothes on. No oil is used, just a little talcum powder to reduce friction, and the pressure is so focused at times it almost borders on painful. When it's over, however, you'll feel absolutely amazing. Good reflexology treatments balance the energy flow of the body, eliminate blood vessel blockage and detox your system. They are particularly good for relieving swollen feet caused by too much heat, or too much shopping. One-hour full-body treatments cost 75 000Rp. *Jl Padma 8X, Legian.* ☎ *(0361) 755 982. No cards.*

❸ ★★★ Jari Menari. Traditional

Balinese massage uses a combination of gentle stretches, acupressure and aromatherapy oils to

Tourists getting massages are a common sight on Kuta Beach.

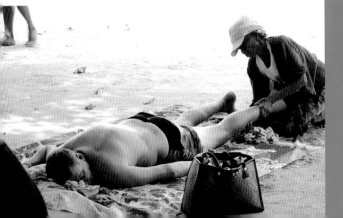

Fish spas are one of the quirkier therapies you'll find in southern Bali.

stimulate the flow of blood, oxygen and 'qi' (energy) around your body, and bring deep relaxation and wellness. One of the best places to experience it is at the spa frequently voted as Bali's number one, Jari Menari, where you can double your indulgence with a four-hands massage by two therapists. (One hour costs 450 000Rp.) Better still, learn how to do it yourself with a full-day massage class every Tuesday from 9am to 3.30pm. It includes a yoga session, hands-on training, lunch and a 90-minute massage, and costs US$170 per person. Book ahead. *See p. 56.*

4 ★ **Fish Spa.** One of the quirkier therapies you'll see in southern Bali is the fish spa. The idea is simple, you put your feet into a tank full of hundreds of hungry little Doctor fish (Garra Rufa fish) and they feast on your dead skin. In reality, it's a very ticklish pedicure. Sometimes you feel a sharp nip, but a twitch of your toe sends them scattering. Your feet will feel lovely afterwards. You'll see tanks in Matahari department store and other popular tourist spots, but head instead to one of the small salons and pay half the price. **We recommend Inggrith Spa** *Jl Laksmana (Jl Oberoi) 22A, Seminyak.* ☎ *(0361) 278 6679. 20-minute treatment 65 000Rp. No cards.*

5 **Jamu Spa School.** If you're really serious about learning the secrets of traditional Indonesian therapies and massage techniques, the Jamu Spa School offers a number of intensive courses, ranging from one-week basic courses to three-month diplomas. Prices start at US$275 per person. *Jl Ngurah Rai Bypass, Tuban.* ☎ *(0361) 704 581. www.jamuspaschool.com.*

6 ★★ **Ubud Yoga Centre.** Yoga is big in Ubud, with lots of resorts offering yoga retreats and classes. The Ubud Yoga Centre not only offers four drop-in classes each day (90 000Rp) but a range of healing programs, such as soul clearing to release your negative karma, Dasa Vayu Healing, which is, apparently (I haven't tried this one), an ancient technique that invites

Yoga is big in Ubud.

The quiet and serene Ubud Botanic gardens are a great place to carry out some contemplation.

cosmic energy into the body to help clear and heal, and all sorts of other energy repairing treatments from 200000Rp to 300000Rp. *Jl Raya Sanggingan, Lungsiakan, Ubud.* ☎ *(0361) 970 460. www. ubudyogacentre.com.*

❼ Sound massage. If you're feeling a bit tender from over-zealous masseurs, the Tibetan Sound massage at Ubud's **Light Spirit** might be just what you need. Brass 'singing' bowls are placed on your body and then 'rung'. The resulting vibrations 'harmonise' your cells, increase your energy and strength, and produce an overall sense of wellbeing. Light Spirit also performs angelic healing (channelling the energy of angels to cleanse your body) but I haven't yet handed over my hard-earned cash to see if it works. *Jl Pengosekan, Ubud.* ☎ *(0361) 857 5570. www.lightspirit bali.com. 45-minute treatment 150000Rp. No cards.*

❽ ★★★ Meditation in the rainforest. The magical meditation court at Ubud's **Botanic Garden** was designed specifically for peace

and quiet, and is the perfect place to carry out some contemplation. *See p. 70.*

❾ ★★ Ubud Sari Health Resort. Forget paying for fancy five-star facilities if all you really want is to detox and get well. Ubud Sari is a no-nonsense health retreat and spa where the focus is on what ails you, not the trimmings. Week-long healing programs are available, or opt for one of the one-day Raw Food and Beauty Sessions. All the food's organic—grown in the fields just across the rice paddies, and the accommodation is actually very nice given the bargain price. *Jl Kajeng 35, Ubud.* ☎ *(0361) 974 393. www.ubud sari.com. Doubles US$60–$75. One-hour massage from US$15. MC, V.*

Travel Tip

You could fill a guidebook just on Bali's multitude of meditation schools, alternative therapies, mystic healers and surf goddess yoga retreats. A good website to find out more is www.balispirit.com.

Foodie Fling

Ubud

SAMBAHAN

UBUD KAJA

Jalan-Sanggingan

Jl. Suweta

Jl. Raya Ubud

Jl. Bisma

Jl. Sandat

Jalan Sayan

Jl. Skukma

UBUD KELOD

Monkey Forest Rd. (Jl. Wenara Wanu)

Sangeh

Ubud

Pejeng

See Ubud inset

Mas

Gianyar

Kapal

Blahbatu

Batuan

Celuk

Sukawati

Ubung

Batubulan

Denpasar

Padang Galak Beach

Kerobokan

Sanur

Sanur Beach

Padma Beach

Seminyak

Legian

Kuta Beach

Kuta

Tuban

Pulau Serangan (Turtle I.)

NGURAH RAI INT'L AIRPORT

Jimbaran Beach

Tanjung Benoa

Jimbaran

Nusa Dua Beach

Teluk Jimbaran

Nusa Dua

Ulu Watu Beach

Ulu Watu

Pecatu

Tg. Mabulu

Green Bali Beach

Nyang Nyang Beach

1. Pasar Badung
2. Snack on Sate Lilit
3. Lunch on Nasi Campur
4. Seafood by the Sea
5. Kopi Luwak
6. Feast on Suckling Pig
7. Dine out on Duck
8. Bubur Injin, Kuta
9. Bubur Injin, Ubud
10. Sate Bali
11. Bumbu Bali, Sanur
12. Bumbu Bali, Ubud

✈ Airport
🏖 Beach

In Bali, food is considered a gift of the gods. It doesn't matter whether your meal is being dished out in paper cones from a roadside cart, being grilled over coconut husks on the beach, served up in a simple *warung* (food stall) or eaten by candlelight in a fancy restaurant, Balinese food is creative, aromatic, colourful and sometimes even sublime. And it doesn't have to cost the earth; some of the best meals I've had in Bali have cost less than US$3. Eat your way across the island. START: **Denpasar produce markets.**

1 ★★★ Pasar Badung. The best way to get know the ingredients of Balinese cuisine is to head to the produce market, and the biggest and best is in Denpasar. *See p. 84.*

2 ★★★ Snack on sate lilit. The ultimate Balinese snack, *sate lilit,* are tasty little sticks of minced fish, pork or chicken mixed with lemongrass, lime, galangal and chilli, grilled over hot charcoal and served with a peanut sauce. You can buy a handful for next to nothing outside the markets in Denpasar, but if you'd rather eat them at a table, try those from **★★★ Made's Warung**. *See p. 130.*

Sate lilit, the ultimate Balinese snack.

3 ★★ Lunch on nasi campur. Most people think *nasi goreng* (fried rice) is Bali's national dish (who can

blame them, you'll find it on every single menu), but it's actually from Java. *Nasi campur,* on the other hand, is the island's true signature dish. Eaten for breakfast, lunch and dinner, it usually includes steamed rice, pork or chicken curry, some fish, tofu or soybean cake, spicy sautéed green vegetables, prawn crackers, egg and a side dish of several sambals. I highly recommend **★★★ Kunyit Bali**. *See p. 129.*

4 ★★★ Seafood by the sea. Eating grilled fish on the beach at Jimbaran Bay may not be the cheapest seafood meal you'll get in Bali, but it is one of the most magical. *See p. 60.* My favourite option is **★ Teba Cafe**. *See p. 134.*

Nasi campur, Bali's true signature dish.

5 ★★★ Kopi Luwak. Indonesia's famous (and famously expensive) cat-poo coffee is made from the beans of coffee berries that have been eaten, digested and defecated by a civet. The resulting coffee is much less bitter than normal coffee and here in Bali it costs a tenth of the price you'd pay elsewhere. Try it at **★★★ Sai Land Coffee Plantation**. *Taman, near Tampaksiring.* ☎ *0859 3518 9140. $*

Bubur Injin: sweet, gooey, and seriously addictive.

6 ★★★ Feast on suckling pig. *Babi guling* is Bali's most special dish, traditionally served at ceremonial feasts. A whole pig is stuffed with chilli, garlic and a host of spices, basted in turmeric and slowly turned on a spit over a fire until it's crisp on the outside and so tender on the inside it melts in your mouth. Remember when I said my best-ever meal cost less than US$3, well, it was a '*spesial*' serve of suckling pig and spiced stuffing doused in a fiery hot sauce and served in a paper cone in Ubud that had my tastebuds tap dancing for days. The memory still makes me go weak at the knees. The place to go is **★★★ Warung Ibu Oka**. *See p. 135.*

7 ★ Dine out on duck. Bali's other great dish is *bebek* or *ayam betutu*, smoked duck or chicken. The birds are stuffed with spices, wrapped in coconut or banana leaves and slowly cooked over glowing coconut husks. Also good is *tum bebek*, juicy little banana leaf parcels of steamed duck that pack a powerful flavour punch. You'll love it at **★★★ Bebek Bengil**. *See p. 123.*

8 9 ★ Bubur Injin. Balinese eat this sweet and gooey pudding for breakfast, but most restaurants serve it as a dessert. It's made with the famous Balinese black rice, palm sugar, grated coconut and coconut milk, and is seriously addictive. You must try it at **★★★ Kafe Batan Waru** in either its Kuta or Ubud locations. *See p. 128.* ●

Cooking Schools

Become a Balinese master chef at one of these cooking schools. Most start with a trip to local markets before the class begins, and finish with one of the best meals you've ever cooked, if you do say so yourself. The following cooking schools are highly recommended: **10 Sate Bali,** (☎ (0361) 736 734; Jl Laksmana (Jl Oberoi) 22A, Seminyak), **11 ★★★ Bumbu Bali** (☎ (0361) 774 502; Jl Pratama, Sanur) and **12 ★ Bumbu Bali** (☎ (0361) 974 217; Jl Suweta 1, Ubud).

Kuta & Legian

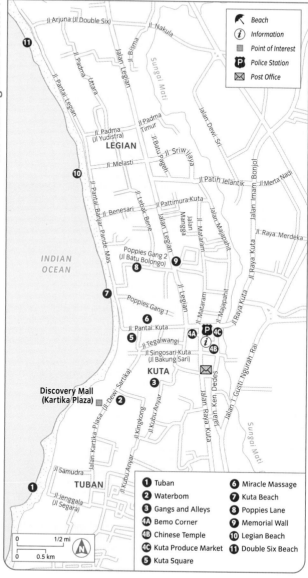

Legend:
- Beach
- (i) Information
- Point of Interest
- P Police Station
- Post Office

Locations:
1. Tuban
2. Waterbom
3. Gangs and Alleys
4A. Bemo Corner
4B. Chinese Temple
4C. Kuta Produce Market
5. Kuta Square
6. Miracle Massage
7. Kuta Beach
8. Poppies Lane
9. Memorial Wall
10. Legian Beach
11. Double Six Beach

Previous page: Pura Ulun Bratan, a temple built on an island in the middle of a lake that's in a volcanic crater, in northern Bali.

Kuta's not for everyone. You either love the round-the-clock party vibe, crowded narrow streets, cheap and colourful sarong shops, loud bars and *warungs* (food stalls) dishing up $2 plates of fried rice; or you can't stand the tattoo shops, crude and rude tourist tat, barrage of hawkers that never leave you alone and constant roar of traffic. Either way, there's no denying Kuta has a spectacular beach. START: **Tuban.**

The Tuban end of Kuta Beach.

1 ★ **Tuban.** The area generally known as Kuta is actually three towns, Tuban, Kuta and Legian, rolled into one, all linked by the beautiful beach. Tuban is the southernmost of the three and it's also the most laid-back (in relative Kuta terms). This section of the beach has fewer hawkers, more fishing, boasts less crowds and, sadly, less sand. But it also has a good shopping centre, some nice beachside bars and resorts, and it can be a good place for children to swim. ⏲ *30 min.*

2 ★★★ **kids Waterbom.** As popular with adults as it is with kids, this water wonderland has water slides, swimming pools, play areas and a swim-up bar. There's a special area for little kids under five and there are always lifeguards on duty. ⏲ *2–4 hr. See p. 27.*

3 ★★★ **Gangs and alleys.** From busy Jl Kartika Plaza (also called Jl Dewi Sartika) head east into the maze of twisting alleyways and narrow lanes, called *gangs*, for a glimpse of real Kuta life. Some of

these paths are so narrow that you and a motorbike won't fit, so if you see one coming, you'll need to find a doorway to flatten yourself against. Don't worry too much about getting lost, just ask someone to point you in the direction of Bemo Corner, but be warned, once away from the tourist hubbub, you'll find the locals so friendly that you need to allow extra time for a chat. ⏲ *30 min.*

4 **Chinese temple & produce markets.** Just before you reach

The maze of twisting alleyways and lanes, called gangs, *give glimpses of real Kuta life.*

The main gates to Kuta Beach.

4A Bemo Corner. Look out for a small **4B Chinese temple.** You'll know you're at Bemo Corner when everybody on the street starts asking you if you need transport. Around the corner from the temple is the main **4C Kuta produce market**. Both spots are your best chance to mix with locals rather than tourists wearing Bintang singlets. If planning to explore the markets, the earlier you can get there the better. ⏱ *30 min. Corner of Jl Blambangan and Jl Raya Kuta.*

5 Kuta Square. This is where you'll find the massive Matahari department store (see p. 147) as well as a range of well-known brands, such as Rip Curl and Just Jeans. ⏱ *10 min.*

6 ★★★ Miracle Massage. If it's your first day in Kuta, you're probably feeling a bit frazzled by the traffic, heat, hawkers, touts and noise by now, so take time out and get a massage. There are literally hundreds of options in Kuta, but I love the guys at Miracle Massage. There's nothing fancy about the room but the fingers of the masseuses here work miracles, and for a fraction of the price of what you'll get in upmarket

spas. Treatments range from 45 000Rp for a one-hour foot reflexology session that includes a wicked neck and shoulder massage to 345 000Rp for three-hour packages with body scrub, facial, cream bath, manicure and pedicure. ⏱ *1 hr. Jl Pantai Kuta.* ☎ *(0361) 758 988.*

7 ★★ Kuta Beach. The main gates to Kuta Beach are at the end of Jl Pantai Kuta, although the actual beach is one continuous 8km stretch of sand from the airport west beyond Seminyak. Take a walk, have a swim and hire a beach chair with umbrella (anywhere between 20 000Rp to 60 000Rp for the day depending on your bargaining skills). Learn to surf, hire a boogie board, and eat fried chicken or fresh fruit from one of the *warungs* under the coconut trees. Get a massage, buy cold beer, ice cream, cheap jewellery, chess sets and sarongs, get your hair braided and have a manicure and pedicure all without leaving your lounge—the world will come to you on Kuta Beach, even if you sometimes wish it would leave you alone. ⏱ *2–3hr.*

8 Poppies Lane. When you tire of the beach make your way up Poppies

Gang II (officially called Jl Batu Bolong). Depending on your point of view, this is the best, or worst, of Kuta, where good times and cheap times converge into one amorphous strip of frenetic and crowded bargain shopping and all-night partying. From the beach it makes a dog-leg past crowded stalls selling cheap sunglasses, wooden penis bottle openers, offensive bumper stickers, 'I love Bali' bags and Bintang singlets, then gets marginally better as it makes its way towards Jl Legian past all-night bars that not only have the 'coldest beer in Bali', but also promise that you'll 'walk in, crawl out'. That said, there are some good little restaurants and some reasonable shops tucked in among it all. ⏱ *45 min.*

The memorial wall, listing the names of the known victims of the terrorist bombings in 2002.

9 Memorial Wall. On Saturday October 12, 2002, 202 people were killed, including 88 Australians, in a terrorist attack on two busy nightclubs on Jl Legian. The memorial wall, built on the site of one of the bomb blasts, lists the names of all the known victims, although it is believed that many more died when they returned injured to their villages unable to get medical attention. It's become a place of pilgrimage, particularly for young Australians. ⏱ *15 min. Jl Legian, opposite Poppies Gang II.*

10 ★★★ Legian Beach. The further west you go along the beach, the quieter it gets and the beachside road is blocked to traffic beyond Jl

Melasti, so it makes for much nicer strolling. Likewise, the shopping and restaurants are of slightly higher quality in Legian compared to Kuta. If you want to lie in the sun without fighting off the attentions of the hawkers, head to Legian. ⏱ *1 hr.*

11 ★★★ Double Six Beach. Popular at night for the nightclubs along its length, during the day Double Six is sleepier even than Legian. This is a good place for sunset drinks, although really, any little beachside bar, often no more than an esky full of cold beer and a couple of plastic chairs plonked on the sand, will do. I recommend **Seaside** for great views and a cocktail list to match. *See p. 133.*

Double Six Beach is a great place for sunset drinks.

Seminyak

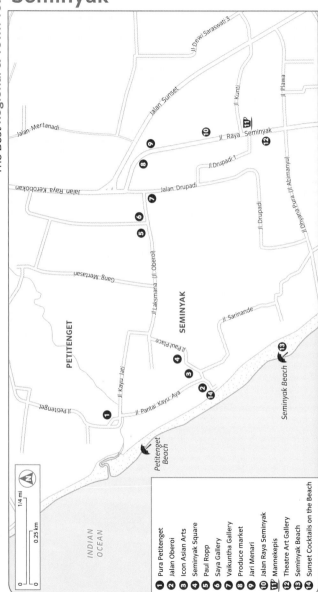

1. Pura Petitenget
2. Jalan Oberoi
3. Icon Asian Arts
4. Seminyak Square
5. Paul Ropp
6. Saya Gallery
7. Vaikuntha Gallery
8. Produce market
9. Jari Menari
10. Jalan Raya Seminyak
11. Mannekepis
12. Theatre Art Gallery
13. Seminyak Beach
14. Sunset Cocktails on the Beach

INDIAN
OCEAN

Petitenget
Beach

Seminyak Beach

PETITENGET

SEMINYAK

Seminyak is Kuta's more sophisticated stylish big sister. It's got the same glorious beach, but less crowds and less hassle, much better restaurants, cocktail bars rather than beer halls and some of the best designer fashion in Bali. Hotels are swanky, the dress code's strict and once the sun goes down everyone glams up. But don't panic if you brought the wrong gear, a day in Seminyak is all about shopping. START: **Pura Petitenget.**

1 ★ Pura Petitenget. Start your tour of Seminyak with a moment of calm contemplation inside this temple, but make sure you have a sarong or the attendants won't let you in. There's often a ceremony happening on the beach opposite, and there's a sign politely asking that you respect the sacredness of the area by swimming further up or down the beach. You might also be lucky enough to be there during a traditional dance competition, where you can watch the gorgeous girls in their colourful costumes gracefully dance across the stage, for free. ⏱ *10 min. Jl Petitenget.*

2 Jalan Oberoi. Walk your way down Jl Oberoi, but don't be perturbed if it's called something else—it also goes by the name of Jl Laksmana and Jl Kayu Aya. As the road twists north you start to enter serious shopping territory: clothes, jewellery and high-end art is the order of the day. ⏱ *15 min (plus shopping time).*

3 ★★★ Icon Asian Arts. This beautiful shop is more like a gallery, showcasing wonderful art and antiques from all over Southeast Asia. If you fall in love with something, you can buy it, but all the pieces are museum quality, so they are not cheap. Looking, however, is free. ⏱ *15 min. Jl Laksmana (Jl Oberoi) 17.*

Pura Petitenget, where ceremonies often take place.

☎ *(0361) 733 875. Daily 11am–7pm. MC, V.*

4 Seminyak Square. There's a collection of shops selling all the high-street brands you can find at home, but on weekends a small market sets up here with stalls selling cheap clothes, shoes and jewellery. Just like Kuta but without the hassle. ⏱ *10 min.*

5 ★★★ Paul Ropp. Even if you'd never dreaming of leaving the house in one of his brightly coloured ensembles, it's worth popping into

Gold masks at Icon Asia Arts, a beautiful shop that is more like a gallery.

this flagship store just to check out the work of one of Bali's most famous fashion designers. *See p. 146.* 🕐 *10 min.*

6 ★ **Saya Gallery.** Zebra-skin thrones, carved wooden spoons, things made with feathers, shells, skin and bone, silver jewellery and glass beads, leather and pearls. It's tribal and quirky, a cornucopia of decorative objets d'art and unexpected treasures. 🕐 *15 min. Jl Laksmana (Jl Oberoi) 12X.* ☎ *(0361) 780 4046. Daily 10am–6pm. MC, V.*

7 **Vaikuntha Gallery.** Five artists, from Bali and Australia, exhibit their work in this little gallery. I love the colourful pop art buddhas printed on plastic rice sacks, but all the work is fresh and modern and quite well priced. 🕐 *10 min. Jl Laksmana (Jl Oberoi) 7.* ☎ *(0361) 736 178. Daily 10am–6pm. No cards.*

8 **Produce market.** Seminyak teems with so many well-dressed beautiful people that it can be easy to forget that the real Bali lurks just below the surface. Get a taste of real life at the local produce market. 🕐 *10 min. Jl Raya Seminyak.*

9 ★★★ **Jari Menari.** This much-lauded spa has been written about in so many magazines that there's hardly enough space left to display them all in the reception area. It likes to boast that it's Bali's best spa, and I'm not about to disagree. Jari Menari means 'dancing fingers', and they really do dance, although if you're shy about being massaged by a male, this place is not for you—the team of therapists is all male. Their speciality treatment is a blend of long massage strokes, rhythmic rocking, gentle stretching and pressure. It is, in a word, bliss. Most treatments cost 300 000Rp to 350 000Rp, and you'll need to book at least 24 hours ahead. 🕐 *60–90 min. Jl Raya Seminyak (Basangkasa) 47.* ☎ *(0361) 736 740. Daily 10am–9pm. MC, V.*

10 **Jalan Raya Seminyak.** Jl Oberoi might be home to fashion and accessories, but Jl Raya Seminyak (also called Jl Raya Basangkasa)

The Theater Art Gallery, a store that is crammed full of puppets, antique pipes, amulets and more.

Seminyak Beach, a splendid stretch of sun, sand and surf.

is full of everything for the home, with lots of lamp shops, basket shops and antique shops—from mirror-encrusted elephant gods to tribal bone carvings and feather headdresses, you'll find it somewhere along this road. There's plenty of designer fashion in among it all as well. ⏻ *30 min (plus shopping time).*

11 ★★ **Mannekepis.** Check out the fish swimming in the ceiling while you wait for your lunch. Good salads and wraps are served here. *See p. 130.*

12 ★★ **Theatre Art Gallery.** A store that feels more like a museum, this one is crammed full of puppets of all descriptions, as well as antique pipes, amulets and 100-year-old Burmese Buddhas. ⏻ *15 min. Jl Raya Seminyak (Basangkasa) 73.* ☎ *(0361) 732 782. Daily 10am–6pm. AE, MC, V.*

13 ★★★ **Seminyak Beach.** Turn right when you get to Jl Dhyana Pura and keep going until you hit the beach. Seminyak's beach is really just a continuation of the same splendid stretch of sun, sand and surf that you get in Kuta, but there's few touts and hawkers and

much less crowds. Even the beachside *warungs* are more upmarket here, with wooden decks and proper chairs. ⏻ *1 hr.*

14 ★★★ **Sunset cocktails on the beach.** Finish off your day with a sundowner and watch the sun sink into the sea at one of the swish restaurants and bars that front the beach. Ku De Ta is my favourite spot, and odds are, it will become yours too. ⏻ *1 hr. See p. 157.*

Sunset cocktails at Ku De Ta are a perfect way to finish off the day.

Bukit Peninsula

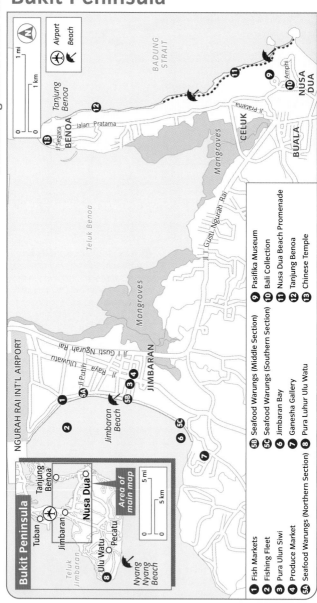

BADING STRAIT

Tanjung Benoa

Jalan Pratama

BENOA

Jl. Segara

Jl. Pratama

CELUK

BUALA

NUSA DUA

Amphi

Teluk Benoa

Mangroves

Mangroves

Jl. I Gusti Ngurah Rai

NGURAH RAI INT'L AIRPORT

Jl. Raya Uluwatu

Jl. Putih

Jl. I Gusti Ngurah Rai

JIMBARAN

Jimbaran Beach

Airport
Beach

1 mi
1 km

Legend

1 Fish Markets
2 Fishing Fleet
3 Pura Ulun Siwi
4 Produce Market
5A Seafood Warungs (Northern Section)
5B Seafood Warungs (Middle Section)
5C Seafood Warungs (Southern Section)
6 Jimbaran Bay
7 Ganesha Gallery
8 Pura Luhur Ulu Watu
9 Pasifika Museum
10 Bali Collection
11 Nusa Dua Beach Promenade
12 Tanjung Benoa
13 Chinese Temple

Bukit Peninsula

Tuban
Tanjung Benoa
Jimbaran
Nusa Dua
Uluwatu
Pecatu
Ulu Watu
Nyang Nyang Beach
Teluk Jimbaran

Area of main map

5 mi
5 km

This ragged tear-shaped peninsula south of Kuta boasts some of the best beaches and coastline in Bali. Jimbaran's near perfect curve of white sand is the place to go for grilled fish on the beach and Ulu Watu's cliff-top temple is one of the most memorable sights in Bali, as long as the cheeky monkeys don't spoil your day with their criminal intent. On the eastern side of the peninsula Nusa Dua offers calm, hassle-free white-sand beaches and lots of family-friendly resorts, or crank up your adrenalin levels with some high-octane water sports in Tanjung Benoa. START: **Jimbaran fish markets.**

① ★★ **Fish Markets.** Jimbaran is famous for its seafood and a visit to the bustling open-air seafood market makes it easy to see why. It's crowded and just a little smelly and full of action. Watch where you step as there are fish scraps and puddles everywhere, and try and keep out of the way of carters scurrying about with large baskets of just-caught fish on their shoulders. Best time to go is in the morning, by mid-afternoon it's all but over. ⏱ *30 min. Jl Pantai Kedonganan.*

② **Fishing Fleet.** Across the road from the fish markets is where the majority of fishing boats pull up, and the beach is a hive of activity as boats come and go, the catch is unloaded and nets are mended. Just offshore the water is crowded with brightly coloured traditional wooden boats. *Kedonganan Beach.*

③ **Pura Ulun Siwi.** This 18th-century temple is worth a look just to get a glimpse of how important the temple is in day to day Balinese life. At any given time its full of gossiping women busily making woven baskets for offerings, or, more often than not, there will be a ceremony in full swing or a gamelan orchestra rehearsal happening. This is one of the only temples in Bali to face east, rather than north to Gunung Agung and the mother temple (see p. 38), believed to be because the temple site dates back the 11th century when the island's spiritual focus was Gunung Semeru across the sea in

Some of the tasty wares on offer at the Jimbaran fish markets.

Colourful traditional fishing boats opposite the Jimbaran fish markets.

Java. There's a sign outside saying you cannot enter unless you are in Balinese traditional dress, but no one seems to mind as long as your legs are covered. ⏱ *10 min. Jl Raya Uluwatu.*

4 Produce Market. Across the road from Pura Ulun Siwi is the produce market, where all kinds of fruit and vegetables are displayed and sold. It's dark and dingy inside, but worth a look just for the exoticness of the produce. The earlier you can go the better, as it's pretty much all over and closed by noon. ⏱ *30 min. Jl Raya Uluwatu.*

5 ★★★ Seafood Warungs. A seafood meal on the beach at Jimbaran is one of the most magical things you will experience in Bali. There are three warung strips each with dozens of almost identical restaurants and cafes spilling across the sand, all charging much the same prices for much the same food, although quality does differ. As the sun sets and the candles are lit, it's a veritable forest of wooden tables as far as the eye can see, and the air is redolent with garlic and heavy with the smoke from the coconut husks that fire the grills. Menu items are charged by weight, but the price includes peanuts with your drinks, rice, a green vegetable, a platter of condiments and fresh fruit for dessert. Expect drinks to be more expensive at night. The 5A northern section is adjacent to the fish market, and tends to be more formal than the other two sections. This is where many of the tour buses will take you, and menu prices are spiked up by around 50% to cover the drivers' or tour guides' commission. Always ask for a local price if you have made your own way there. The 5B middle section is a little more basic, and marginally cheaper. The 5C southern section, near the Four Seasons Resort, is the best pick of the three, and the only one that isn't completely deserted at lunch time. If dining at high tide, watch out for your shoes and handbags left on the sand as the waves often lap at the table legs. And beware of taxi scam artists that will try and tell you there is minimum charge for the local area, at around three times the metered rate. If staying in the local area, many restaurants will pick you up and take you home.

6 ★★★ Jimbaran Bay. The long curve of golden sand stretches from the airport south to the Four Seasons Resort, and although different sections have different names, such as Kedonganan near the fish markets and Muaya in the south, it's all just one long beach. The waves can be real dumpers very close to shore and there are strong undertows, so always swim in a patrolled section. Best spot to get wet is down the southern end, which is also where you'll find plenty of wannabe and first-time surfers. ⏱ *1–3 hr.*

7 ★ Ganesha Gallery. Most galleries inside five-star resorts tend to be mere showrooms geared for sales to well-heeled tourists, but the Ganesha Gallery inside the Four Seasons Resort is worth a look if you are into contemporary art. There are changing exhibitions by well-known local and international artists, and the calibre is very high. ⏱ *15 min. Jl Four Seasons Resort. Free admission.*

8 ★★★ Pura Luhur Ulu Watu. One of the most visually arresting temples in Bali, Ulu Watu sits on the very edge of a vertiginous cliff on the southern coast of the Bukit Peninsula. Even if temples bore you

silly, you should still go here just to see the see-forever views and meet the delinquent monkeys. Many people visit on a sunset tour, but charter a taxi or hire a car or bike and head out in the early morning when the place is deserted and the monkeys are still half asleep and less likely to steal your sunglasses. Approximate one-way taxi fare from Jimbaran to Ulu Watu is around 70 000Rp to 80 000Rp depending on traffic; your driver will often wait for you for the return ride if you just want to make a morning trip out of it. See p. 35. ⏱ *1 hr.*

9 ★★★ Pasifika Museum. I can't quite work out why this museum is always empty, given its extensive art collection. Most of it is painted by Balinese, or paintings of Bali and Balinese by visiting Asian and Western artists. All the big names are here, including Donald Fried, Arie Smit, Theo Meier and Adrien Le Mayeur. For those who don't really fancy room after room of art, the Pacific Room has a fantastic collection of carvings, masks, canoes, jewellery, and all sorts of artefacts from across the Pacific, particularly Vanuatu and Papua New Guinea, and is worth the price of

A meal at a seafood warung on Jimbaran beach is a magical experience.

Pura Luhur Ulu Watu, one of the most visually arresting temples in Bali.

admission alone. ⏲ *1 hr. Bali Collection, Block P.* ☎ *(0361) 774 624. Admission 70 000Rp. Daily 10am–6pm.*

⑩ Bali Collection. Across the road from Pasifika Museum is the Bali Collection, a rather sterile rabbit warren of Western-brand shops, a restaurant and a department store. The doors are all open but there's hardly ever anyone here shopping. I'd only bother if you are in desperate need of retail therapy or it's been raining so long you've run out of other options. There are shuttle buses that will run you to and from your hotel (or close by) at regular intervals, but if you want to travel outside these times, the taxis at the shopping centre will charge you triple the metered rate—walk up through the gates to the main road (around five minutes) and hail a metered taxi.

⑪ ★ Nusa Dua Beach Promenade. This 5km paved pathway runs the length of the beach from just south of the Bali Collection almost all the way to Tanjung Benoa, past all the beachside resorts. It's perfect for an early morning walk or jog, or late afternoon stroll. ⏲ *1–2 hr.*

The Pasifika Museum, a blissfully uncrowded place with a fantastic collection of art and artefacts.

The Chinese temple, a riot of gold paint, red and yellow paper lanterns and crouching dragons.

⑫ Tanjung Benoa. Nusa Dua is a gated community of beachside resorts, and while they are nice enough to stay in, it can be easy to forget you are in Bali. An afternoon spent in Tanjung Benoa will remind you where you are, and at least offer a modicum of local shopping and inexpensive eating that you won't find in the resorts. Benoa's harbour is crammed with fishing boats, jet skis and speed boats of all descriptions, eager to tow thrill-seeking tourists behind them on a parasail, banana boat or flying fish. ⏱ *1 hr. See p. 63.*

⑬ Chinese Temple. Benoa has a sizeable Chinese population, and the Chinese temple is a riot of gold paint, red and yellow paper lanterns and crouching dragons. This end of town near the harbour on the very tip of the peninsula is the poster child for multidenominationalism; if you head left around the corner, you'll find a mosque, or go right for a Hindu temple, all happily co-existing within metres of each other. ⏱ *15 min. Jl Segara Lor.*

Take to the skies over the beach at Tanjung Benoa.

Sanur

1. Beach Market
2. Museum Le Mayeur
3. Beach Promenade
4. Kite Surfing
5. Fishing Boats
6. Woodwork Market
7. Stiff Chilli
8. Stone Pillar
9. Gardens at Bali Hyatt
10. Gudang Keramik
11. Nogo Bali Ikat Centre
12. Jamu Spa

Beach
Police Station
Post Office

Sanur has a little of everything, in just the right amounts. A gorgeous white-sand beach, one of the best beachside walks in Bali, beachfront hotels, enough shops and market stalls to keep even the most ardent shopper happy and plenty of laid-back seaside dining and cheap on-the-sand bars. In short, Sanur's everything you love about Bali, without the hassle, hustle, traffic and crowds.
START: **Northern end of the beach promenade, near Jalan Hang Tuah.**

1 Beach Market. There's a small market selling sarongs and other souvenirs on the edge of the sand near the beginning of the 4km-long beach promenade.

2 ★★★ Museum Le Mayeur. Belgian artist Adrien Le Mayeur lived in Sanur during the 1930s until 1958. His paintings of Balinese life have an ethereal, garden-of-Eden-like quality, many of them depicting his dancer wife, Ni Pollack, and scenes of daily Balinese life long vanished. His house is now a museum and around 80 of his works, including a number of impressionistic European scenes, are displayed here, as well as some stunning black and white photos of Pollack. The house alone is reason enough to visit, it's a typical, but exquisite, example of traditional Balinese architecture, with carved stone walls on the outside and richly decorated red and gold wooden carving inside, and quite a lot of original furniture. The gardens are also delightful. ⏲ *1 hr. Jl Hang Tuah Pantai (Beach Promenade), Sanur.* ☎ *(0361) 286 201. Admission 5000Rp. Daily 8.30am–4pm, except Friday 8.30am–12.30pm.*

3 ★★★ Beach Promenade. The 4km-long paved walkway follows the curve of Sanur's long protected beach, and is one of my favourite coastal walks in Bali. You'll occasionally get asked if you'd like a massage or to check out the selection of sarongs in someone's stall, but it's delightfully hassle free and has plenty of places to stop for a bite to eat or a cold drink along the way. ⏲ *1–2 hr.*

4 Kite surfing. Sanur might be famous for its high-flying kites (see 'Flying High', p. 67), but it's also one of the best places in Bali to fly a different type of kite, one that will propel you across the waves faster than a speeding bullet. Kite surfing

Museum Le Mayeur, a typical, but exquisite, example of traditional Balinese architecture.

lessons and rental are available at the Bali Kite Centre at the Inna Grand Bali Beach Hotel. ⏱ *2 hr.* ☎ *(0361) 276 6665. www.bali kitecenter.com.*

5 Fishing boats. South of the Bali Hyatt the beach begins to narrow, and paddling tourists are replaced by local fishermen in conical hats (and the occasional bike helmet) wielding fishing rods as they stand waist deep in the water. Here the shore is lined with colourful fishing boats, and groups of fishermen sit chatting in the shade of coconut trees mending their nets or tending their boats. ⏱ *10 min.*

6 Woodwork Market. This small collection of stalls is full of wooden carvings. Most are touristy, but you'll find the occasional good one if you spend enough time looking and the prices are reasonable. ⏱ *10 min.*

7 Stiff Chilli. You deserve a break, and a treat, after your 4km beach walk, so order a coffee, or a gelato, and take 10 gazing out to sea or watching the squirrels scurry up and down the trees. *See p. 133.*

Sanur beach is one of the best locations in Bali for kite surfing.

The beachfront promenade at Sanur, a beautiful coastal walk.

8 Stone Pillar. Bali's oldest dated artefact is a remnant of a stone pillar covered in Sanskrit inscriptions recounting military events from more than a thousand years ago. You'll find it behind glass in the courtyard of slightly shabby Pura Belanjong, just off Jl Danau Poso, but there are no explanations in English, so unless you know your Sanskrit it can be a slightly underwhelming experience. ⏱ *10 min.*

9 ★★ Gardens at Bali Hyatt. Sanur is a green and leafy place, and walking the streets can be a pleasurable experience thanks to the abundance of shade—although, like everywhere in Bali, some footpaths would be nice. If you're a garden lover, or just in need of some green space, take a stroll around the extensive gardens of the Bali Hyatt. ⏱ *30 min. Jl Danau Tamblingan.* ☎ *(0361) 281 234. www.bali. resort.hyatt.com.*

10 ★ Gudang Keramik. Lovely ceramic tableware at bargain prices. Designs are bold and simple with lots of primary colours and technically they're all seconds, but in most cases you'd never know. ⏱ *15 min. Jl Danau Tamblingan.* ☎ *(0361) 289 363. MC, V.*

11 ★ Nogo Bali Ikat Centre. All of the fabrics are handwoven in this lovely shop, although I suspect the

Flying High

Flying a kite is a favourite pastime of Balinese—young and old—particularly in the dry, windy months of June, July and August. But kite flying is considered an art form in Sanur, and every year, around late July and early August, hundreds of kite makers and flyers compete in the Bali Kite Festival. Bigger is definitely better—some kites are up to 10m high with a tail that stretches more than 100m, and some fly so high that if you were a pilot you'd be on the lookout.

loom out the front is mainly for show. The fabric and clothing range manages to be both traditional and contemporary at the same time, and this is a good place to pick up a unique piece of Balinese design. ⏱ *15 min. Jl Danau Tamblingan 104.* ☎ *(0361) 288 765. AE, MC, V.*

🔟② ★★★ **Jamu Spa.** Indulge in a traditional body treatment or massage at this beautiful spa. The signature treatment is the two-hour Ocean Detox, which includes a massage followed by a body scrub made from seaweed and sea salt crystals (US$80), but if you don't have time

South of the Bali Hyatt, the beach becomes less touristy and fishermen are a common sight.

for that, try the half-hour rose petal eye mask (US$30). ⏱ *1–2 hr. Jl Danau Tamblingan 41.* ☎ *(0361) 286 595. AE, MC, V.*

A weaver at work at the Nogo Bali Ikat Centre.

Ubud

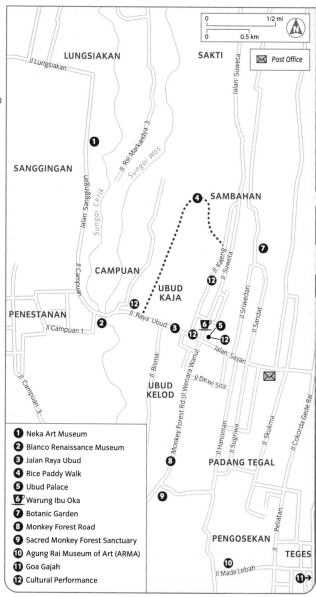

1 Neka Art Museum
2 Blanco Renaissance Museum
3 Jalan Raya Ubud
4 Rice Paddy Walk
5 Ubud Palace
6 Warung Ibu Oka
7 Botanic Garden
8 Monkey Forest Road
9 Sacred Monkey Forest Sanctuary
10 Agung Rai Museum of Art (ARMA)
11 Goa Gajah
12 Cultural Performance

I have never met anyone who hasn't fallen in love with Ubud. Bali's cultural capital is a collection of villages that cling to the hillsides and edges of jungle-clad river gorges, surrounded by rice paddies so green they'll hurt your eyes. Ubud moves to a much gentler pace than the tourist towns of the south, although that doesn't mean the traffic is any better, but the shopping and eating certainly is. It might be a cliché, but it's kind of true—Ubud is the real Bali.

START: **Neka Art Museum, just west of Ubud.**

❶ ★★★ Neka Art Museum.
Ubud has more museums and art galleries than any other place in Bali, but if you only see one, make it the Neka. The focus is on Balinese art, but the photos of Kuta before it became a tourist fleshpot and the collection of kris (ceremonial daggers) also displayed are worth the price of admission even if art isn't really your thing. 🕐 *90 min. See p. 31.*

❷ ★★★ Blanco Renaissance Museum.
The beautiful gardens, exotic birds and flamboyant style of the Dali of Bali make this another art museum that has so much more than just paintings on the wall. 🕐 *30–45 min. See p. 32.*

❸ Jalan Raya Ubud.
One of Ubud's main streets has plenty to see, including two of my favourite temples, Pura Taman Saraswati and Pura Dalem (see p. 37), and the Museum Puri Lukisan (see p. 32), but it also has some great antique stores where you can pick up tribal and ethnic carvings, sculptures and jewellery from all over Indonesia. 🕐 *30–45 min.*

❹ ★★★ Rice paddy walk.
You only ever have to walk a block or two away from the shopping streets in Ubud before you'll be surrounded by terraced rice paddies. There's a lovely little walk that loops around the north side of Jl Raya Ubud. Easiest way to find it is to walk up Jl Kajeng past the Ubud Sari Health Resort and just follow the track as it

A rice farmer at work in a rice paddy near Ubud.

leads through the paddies. You'll come back out on Jl Raya Ubud not far from the Pura Dalem. Watch out for mud, and the occasional snake. 🕐 *30 min.*

❺ ★★ Ubud Palace.
Ubud has always been ruled by royalty, and while they might not wield much power these days, there's still a royal family in residence at the palace. You can't see inside, but you can wander around the courtyard and admire the carved gates and doorways. It's a great place to see a cultural performance. 🕐 *10 min. Corner of Jl Raya Ubud and Jl Suweta. Admission free. See p. 156.*

❻ ★★★ Warung Ibu Oka.
Don't even think about leaving Ubud without trying some of the best suckling pig in Bali. *See p. 135.*

The gates at the Ubud Palace, where a royal family still resides.

7 ★★★ **Botanic Garden.** You could spend all day sitting quietly in this gorgeous garden (I've been known to) with its meandering creeks, rainforest gully, silent mediation court, love nest (follow the signs), bamboo grove and orchid garden, and that's without getting lost in the maze. It's 2km north of Ubud—a motorbike taxi will cost

Get lost in the hedge maze in the Ubud Botanic garden.

around 10000Rp each way, or catch a ride there and walk back down the gentle slope through the rice paddies. ⏱ *1–2 hr. Jl Tirta Tawar.* ☎ *(0361) 970 951. Admission 50000Rp. Daily 8am–6pm.*

8 **Monkey Forest Road.** All roads lead to the monkey forest, or so it seems. Both Monkey Forest Road (officially Jl Wenara Wana) and Jl Hanoman end up there, and both are lined with galleries, artist's studios, boutiques, jewellery stores, handicraft shops and cafes. Shop till you drop, but if you are planning on walking through the forest, you'll need to keep any purchases out of reach of the monkeys. ⏱ *20 min.*

9 ★★ **kids Sacred Monkey Forest Sanctuary.** There's nothing sacred about the monkeys—they are thieving little imps, but they do have the most adorable faces that are impossible not to love, even if they have just stolen your brand-new sunglasses (lucky they only cost US$5) or pulled the bag of peanuts out of your pocket and run off. The monkeys are the drawcard, but I love coming here just to walk thought the cool jungle with its riverside trails, super-sized banyan trees and moss-covered temples. ⏱ *1 hr. Jl Wenara Wana.* ☎ *(0361) 971 304. Admission 20 000Rp. Daily 8am–6pm.*

⑩ ★★ Agung Rai Museum of Art (ARMA). Wander through the gardens, take an art class or catch a traditional dance performance. ⏱ *1 hr. See p. 33.*

⑪ ★★ Goa Gajah. I'm not sure why it's called the Elephant Cave—there are no native elephants in Bali and the massive demon face carved around the entrance to the cave looks nothing like an elephant. Maybe there was a good reason back in the 11th century when the cave was first in use. The actual cave itself is tiny, and there are two even smaller shrines inside. It would all be a bit of an anticlimax if it wasn't for the bathing pools, where if you splash the water coming out of the fountains on your face you'll get good luck, and the lovely little trek through the jungle to the ruined remains of a Buddhist temple. ⏱ *1 hr. Jl Bedulu, 5km east of Ubud*

The entrance to Goa Gajah, a tiny cave with shrines inside.

(catch a taxi). Admission 15 000Rp. Daily 8am–6pm.

⑫ ★★★ Cultural Performance. Watching a Kecak trance dance by firelight in a temple courtyard is an experience not to be missed. Ubud is the best place to catch a show and there's usually one being performed in a temple somewhere every night of the week. ⏱ *2 hr. See p. 157.*

Two residents of the Sacred Monkey Forest Sanctuary.

Bali High

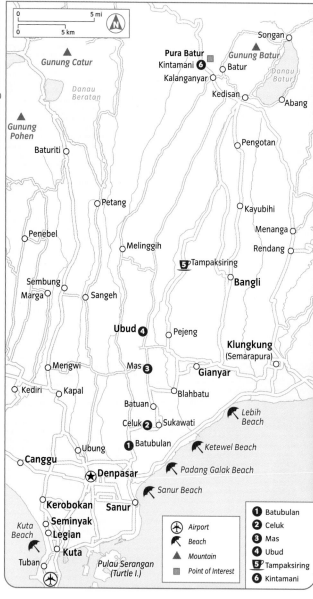

✈	Airport
🏖	Beach
▲	Mountain
■	Point of Interest

❶	Batubulan
❷	Celuk
❸	Mas
❹	Ubud
5	Tampaksiring
❻	Kintamani

Bali may have a spiritual heart, but her backbone is a ridge of mountain peaks and volcanic cones. Considered both holy and all powerful, the last eruptions were just a few years ago. Escape the coastal heat and take a day trip through artisan villages into the mist-shrouded central highlands. START: **Kuta, Seminyak, Jimbaran, Nusa Dua or Sanur.**

① Batubulan. The road leading to Batubulan is lined with a forest of Buddhas, most bound for export. Search around, though, and you'll find plenty of Hindu temple gods and other beautiful creations made from the soft volcanic stone. Batubulan is also one of the main centres for batik production. ⏱ *30 min. See p. 142.*

② Celuk. The silversmiths of Celuk make the best jewellery in Bali. ⏱ *30 min. See p. 24, bullet* **⑪**.

③ Mas. Despite Mas being the Indonesian word for gold, it's wood that the artisans of Mas make their living from, carving anything and everything from temple decorations and life-sized horses, pigs and cows to beautiful furniture and masks. ⏱ *30 min.*

④ Ubud. You could spend a week in Ubud and not get bored, with shopping, hidden temples in the jungle, art galleries, museums, sacred forests full of monkeys and beautiful rice paddies. ⏱ *2 hr. For more details, see p. 68 and p. 30.*

Gunung Batur's crater lake.

A batik maker, hard at work.

⑤ ★★★ Tampaksiring. If you are hankering after a good cup of coffee, head straight to the source, one of the coffee plantations in the hills north of Ubud. If you've ever wanted to try the insanely expensive Kopi Luwak, which retails for A\$50 a cup in Australia, you can get some for around 30 000Rp (around US\$4) at Sai Land Coffee Plantation in the village of Taman near Tampaksiring. ⏱ *30 min. See p. 48.*

⑥ ★★ Kintamani. The hawkers are aggressive but if you can ignore them the views of Gunung Batur, Bali's second-highest volcano, and its double caldera and crater lake are awesome, especially if you are lucky enough to be here on a day without clouds. Its last major eruption was in 1994 and you can still see the black scars left by the lava flow. ⏱ *30 min. For details on trekking and temples in the area, see p. 38 and p. 93.*

Eastern Bali

0 — 5 mi
0 — 5 km

Gunung Agung

4

3 Besakih

Kayubihi

Menanga

Rendang

Muncan

Bebandem

Pulung

Sibetan

Sidemen

2

Klungkung
(Semarapura)

1

Kusamba

Padangbai
Kusamba Beach
Beach

BADUNG
STRAIT

Culik

Amed

Amed
Beach

Bunutan

Tista

Gunung Seraya

Seraya Timur

5

Seraya

Amlapura

6

9 Tenganan

Bugbug

8

Candidasa

Teluk
Amuk

Padangbai

7 Whitesand Beach

10

🏄 Beach

▲ Mountain

1 Taman Kertha Gosa	**6** Taman Ajung
2 Sideman Road	**7** Pasir Putih
3 Pura Besakih	**8** Candidasa
4 Gunung Agung	**9** Tenganan
5 Taman Tirta Gangga	**10** Pura Goa Lawah

Ancient kingdoms, grand palaces and holy temples. Eastern Bali may not have the beautiful white-sand beaches and rolling surf of the south, but there's plenty here that rewards a few days' exploration. Base yourself in the sleepy seaside town of Candidasa and uncover a more regal side of Balinese life. START: **Semarapura.**

1 ★★ Taman Kertha Gosa.

Before the arrival of the Dutch, Semarapura (Klungkung) was one of Bali's most important kingdoms, and the remains of the grand palace here (the majority of it was destroyed by the Dutch in 1908) are some of the finest in the country. Highlights include the Hall of Justice, with its intricately painted ceiling showing mythological scenes, and the Floating Pavilion, which also has a painted ceiling. At the back of the complex is a small museum with some evil-looking kris (ceremonial daggers) and other ceremonial

The painted ceiling at Taman Kertha Gosa, the grand palace of one of Bali's most important kingdoms before the arrival of the Dutch.

Gunung Agung, Bali's highest and most venerated mountain, which is actually still an active volcano.

items, and some great photos of the court in all its splendour. There's also an exhibition of paintings and sculptures by Emilio Ambron, an Italian artist who lived in Bali in the late 1930s and early 40s. ⏱ *1 hr. Jl Puputan, Semarapura. Admission 12000Rp. Daily 7am–6pm.*

② ★★★ **Sideman Road.** Heading up to Besakih via Sideman Road may not be the most direct route, but it's worth the slight detour for the stunning rice paddy scenery along the way. ⏱ *30 min.*

③ ★★ **Pura Besakih.** It's crowded and full of people trying to relieve you of your hard-earned cash, but even so, a visit the 'Mother Temple' is still worthwhile, so long as you're not expecting a spiritual experience. ⏱ *90 min.* See p. 38.

④ **Gunung Agung.** Pura Besakih is halfway up Bali's highest and most venerated mountain. It's actually a volcano, still active, and is 3142m high, although that changes with each eruption; the last major one was in 1964. It's a popular trekking spot (see p. 23), but you'll need to be lucky to see the summit as it's usually obscured by clouds. If it's a fine day, you can get a good view from the temple, but best views are usually seen from the northern side.

⑤ ★★★ **Taman Tirta Gangga.** The last rajah of Karangasem had a water fetish and built two over-the-top water palaces. His first was south of Amlapura (see p. 76, bullet **⑥**), but it was his second at Tirta Gangga where he really let his aquatic vision fly. Built on the site of a holy spring (and named after the Ganges River in India), it is an aquatic playground of pools, ponds and fountains surrounded by beautiful gardens. There are two pools where you can swim, although one is for ritualistic

Pura Besakih, the 'Mother Temple'.

Taman Tirta Gangga, an aquatic playground surrounded by beautiful gardens.

bathing only. Bring a picnic lunch and you could stay here all day. ⏱ *1 hr. Admission 5000Rp, swimming 6000Rp extra. Daily 6am–6pm.*

⑥ Taman Ajung. Not nearly as ornate as Tirta Gangga, this water palace, built in 1921, destroyed by earthquake in 1979 and since rebuilt, features lots of pavilions and expanses of water, but lacks the vitality and chaotic charm of Tirta Gangga. There are good views of the palace grounds from the hill above; I wouldn't bother going inside unless you've got a particular interest. ⏱ *5 min. Admission 5000Rp. Daily 6am–6pm.*

⑦ ★ Pasir Putih. Most of this section of the coast has black-sand beaches, but just north of Candidasa, a hand-painted sign in the village of Perasi points down a ridiculously rough road that leads you to a beautiful crescent of white sandy beach. ⏱ *Half a day.*

⑧ ★★ Candidasa. You don't come to Candidasa for the nightlife, or the surf, or even really the beach, although it is beside the sea. Sadly, most of the sand has been washed away, thanks to the mining of the offshore reefs in the 1980s. Breakwalls have been built and the beach is slowly returning, but you can't really walk the length of them because in some places hotel walls drop straight into the sea. Despite all this, I love Candidasa for its relaxed attitude and easygoing nature. At the northern end of the beach is a fishing village where you'll find fishing boats, coconut trees, and chickens and piglets rooting around the gardens. In the middle section is a beautiful lily-covered lagoon. If you want to swim, paddle or hire a boat, head to the southern section, where you'll also find some cheap *warungs* serving up just-caught fish.

⑨ ★★★ Tenganan. The Bali Aga people are the original Balinese, inhabitants of the island long before the Javanese Majapahits arrived in the 11th century. Tenganan is a Bali Aga village, famous for

The lily-covered lagoon at Candidasa.

An artisan creating hand-woven ikat *cloth at Tenganan.*

its traditional arts and crafts, particularly the finely woven baskets (you can find them in boutiques in Seminyak and Ubud), hand-woven *ikat* cloth and *lontar* (palm leaf) books. There's no denying the village is touristy, especially if you arrive at the same time as a tour bus, but it's is still worth visiting. Chat to the artisans for more than a minute and you'll most likely be invited into their homes (many of which double as shops) where you will get a rare glimpse of traditional life. It's the perfect opportunity to pick up a souvenir, and at least your know your money is going directly to the person who made it. Leave your credit card at home, it's cash only. ⏱ *1 hr. Admission into the village is by donation. A motorbike taxi from Candidasa will cost around 15000Rp each way.*

🔟 **Pura Goa Lawah.** There's no mystery why they call this the Bat Cave Temple. The cave in the cliff face is home to thousands, maybe millions, of bats—and a few snakes.

Legend has it that the cave leads to Pura Goa (Cave Temple) within the Besakih temple complex 20km away. I'm pretty sure the stink would drive you to distraction long before you got there. ⏱ *15 min. Admission 10000Rp. Daily 8am–6pm.*

The finished product of a Bali Aga artisan's work.

Northern Bali

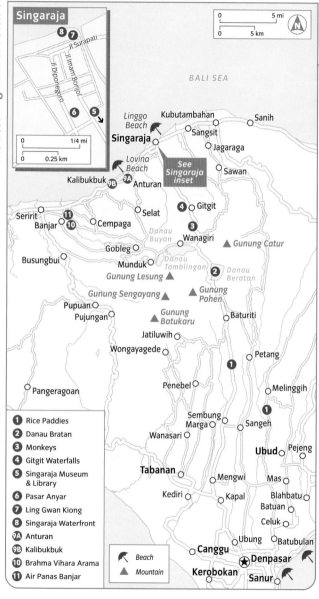

Singaraja

Jl Surapati
Jl Imam Bonjol
Jl Diponegoro

0   1/4 mi
0   0.25 km

0   5 mi
0   5 km

BALI SEA

Linggo Beach
Singaraja
Kubutambahan
Sanih
Sangsit
Jagaraga
Sawan

Lovina Beach
Kalibukbuk
Anturan
See Singaraja inset
Gitgit

Seririt
Banjar
Cempaga
Selat
Wanagiri
Gunung Catur

Busungbui
Gobleg
Danau Buyan
Munduk
Danau Tamblingan
Danau Beratan
Gunung Lesung ▲
Gunung Sengayang ▲
Gunung Pohen ▲

Pupuan
Pujungan
Gunung Batukaru ▲
Baturiti

Jatiluwih
Wongayagede
Petang

Pangeragoan
Penebel
Melinggih

Sembung
Marga
Sangeh
Wanasari

Ubud
Pejeng

Tabanan
Mengwi
Mas
Kediri
Kapal
Blahbatu
Batuan
Celuk

Ubung
Batubulan
Canggu
Denpasar ★
Kerobokan
Sanur

1 Rice Paddies
2 Danau Bratan
3 Monkeys
4 Gitgit Waterfalls
5 Singaraja Museum & Library
6 Pasar Anyar
7 Ling Gwan Kiong
8 Singaraja Waterfront
9A Anturan
9B Kalibukbuk
10 Brahma Vihara Arama
11 Air Panas Banjar

🏖 Beach
▲ Mountain

Lovina is chalk to Kuta's cheese. Laid-back, quiet and very low-key, this is what Kuta might once have been, but with volcanic black sand and minus the rolling waves. Hotels are shabby and cheap and almost all front the beach, and the seafood at seaside *warungs* is half the price you'd pay at Jimbaran. Getting here's half the fun, and once you're here, kick back, relax and do nothing much at all. START: **Ubud**

Pura Ulun Bratan, an island temple.

1 ★ Rice paddies. It only takes a few minutes on the road north of Ubud towards Payangan and Bedugul before you are surrounded by beautiful green rice paddies. Just 15 minutes later and you know you've left the tourist trail as you wind through tiny villages, wait for temple processions to pass by and enjoy traffic-free roads. If only driving in Bali was always this free and easy.

2 ★★ Danau Bratan. To get to Lovina and the north coast first you must cross the spine of mountains in the middle of Bali, so get ready for some winding roads, stunning scenery and cool mountain air (most likely in the form of mist). Stop at one of the roadside stalls for a punnet of sweet strawberries and visit Pura Ulun Bratan, built on an island in the middle of the lake, which is actually in the middle of an extinct volcano. On weekends and afternoons it can get a bit crowded; early morning is magical when the temple is shrouded in mist. ⏱ *45 min. Admission 10 000Rp.*

3 Monkeys. You'll know you have reached the summit when you start seeing monkeys by the side of the road. It's all downhill from here, and you'll soon start seeing coastal views.

4 Gitgit waterfalls. Around halfway down the winding mountain road, Gitgit is home to two waterfalls, the first a multitiered cascade,

Singaraja's chaotic and colourful produce market.

The Yudha Mandala Tama monument, on the Singaraja waterfront.

the second, Air Terjun Gitgit, a 40m-high waterfall. Both are popular with tour groups and you'll often have to fight your way through the buses and sarong sellers, but the waterfalls are refreshing on a hot day, although the amount of litter is depressing. ⏱ *30 min. Admission 6000Rp.*

⑤ ★ Singaraja Museum & Library. Singaraja may be Bali's second-largest city but it's not a tourist town, and it shows in the general shabbiness of its one and only museum, the Museum Buleleng, which has some dusty archaeological exhibits and a room with some images of the local rajahs in the 1930s. Much more interesting is the small library next door, which has an extensive collection of *lontar* books made from dried palm leaves. There's hardly ever anyone there, so you'll probably need to turn on the lights—and turn them off again when you leave. ⏱ *15 min. Jl Veteran.* ☎ *(0361) 22645. Free admission. Mon–Thurs 8am–4pm, Fri 8am–1pm.*

⑥ ★★ Pasar Anyar. Singaraja's chaotic and colourful produce market is a crowded warren of woven baskets overflowing with fruit and vegetables and stalls selling all manner of amazing and exotic food stuffs, some of which I'd never seen before. ⏱ *30 min. Jl Diponegoro.*

⑦ ★ Ling Gwan Kiong. Singaraja has a sizeable Chinese population and its colourful waterfront temple dates back to 1873. Watch where you step, the temple turtles have a habit of escaping. ⏱ *10 min. On the waterfront off Jl Erlangga.*

Bali's only Buddhist monastery, Brahma Vihara Arama.

8 ★ Singaraja Waterfront. Take a walk along the old harbour waterfront, past the impressive Yudha Mandala Tama monument commemorating the independence struggle against the Dutch. Look around and you can still see traces of the colonial past in much of the architecture; Singaraja was the capital of Bali under Dutch colonial rule. ⏱ *15 min.*

9 ★★★ Lovina. The area known as Lovina is actually two seaside villages around 5km apart, **9A Anturan** and **9B Kalibukbuk**. Anturan is around 5km west of Singaraja and the quieter of the two, although that's not saying much because the centre of Lovina, Kalibukbuk, is hardly action central. Beaches have black sand and waves are few, but it's a wonderful place to laze around and chill out while making friends with the locals and eating grilled fish that was flapping around in the bottom of the boat on the sand beside your table only minutes ago. You can go dolphin watching in the morning (you can't miss the dolphin monument on the beach at Kalibukbuk), but the flotilla of buzzing boats chasing a few harried creatures around the bay borders on dolphin harassment. You can also take dive and snorkelling trips to the west coast. *See p. 23.*

The dolphin monument at Kalibukbuk.

10 ★★★ Brahma Vihara Arama. Bali's only Buddhist monastery is a mini Borobudur, full of grey stone stupas and an overriding sense of calm, although there are plenty of Hindu touches as well. There's usually some sort of meditation session going on (hence the peace and quiet) and visitors are free to join in. The views towards the coast are lovely. You'll need a sarong. ⏱ *30 min. Admission by donation.*

11 ★★★ Air Panas Banjar. Surrounded by lush jungle-like gardens, these hot springs are guaranteed to relax you. Thankfully, given the climate, they are more tepid than hot, but they still provide a wonderful soak. There are two pools that cascade into each other. The top one is warmer and you can massage out any neck or shoulder kinks under the gushing demon-head fountains. For a real pounding, head to a third pool where the water pours down from 3m-high spouts. ⏱ *1 hr. Admission 5000Rp. Daily 8am–6pm.*

The hot springs at Air Panas Banjar.

Central Denpasar

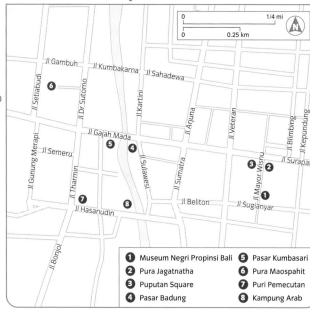

0   1/4 mi
0   0.25 km

Jl Gambuh   Jl Kumbakarna   Jl Sahadewa
Jl Setiabudi
Jl Dr Sutomo
Jl Kartini
Jl Arjuna
Jl Veteran
Jl Blimbing
Jl Kepundung
Jl Gajah Mada
Jl Surapati
Jl Gunung Merapi
Jl Semeru
Jl Mayor Wisnu
Jl Sulawesi
Jl Sumatra
Jl Tharmin
Jl Beliton   Jl Sugianyar
Jl Hasanudin
Jl Bonjol

1. Museum Negri Propinsi Bali   5. Pasar Kumbasari
2. Pura Jagatnatha   6. Pura Maospahit
3. Puputan Square   7. Puri Pemecutan
4. Pasar Badung   8. Kampung Arab

I f you want to get a sense of the real workaday modern
Bali, head to the capital Denpasar. Resolutely ignored by most
visitors to the island, the city is well worth a look, and despite its
(deserved) reputation as a sprawling, traffic-choked metropolis
you can see the best of the sights on an easy one-day walking tour.
And you won't see a Bintang singlet all day. START: **Museum Negri
Propinsi Bali.**

**1 ★★ Museum Negri Propinsi
Bali.** Established by the Dutch in
1910 this museum, a former palace
set in beautiful gardens, showcases
not only traditional Balinese architecture but also the arts and rituals
of Bali, and is a good introduction
to Balinese culture. There are four
pavilions, the first focusing on
archaeological artefacts, many
ancient. Upstairs is a room of Balinese fine art tracing its various
movements and evolution from early
temple art through to contemporary
works. The performing arts pavilion
houses dance costumes and masks,
including a fearsome looking Barong
lion used in one of Bali's most popular dances. A third pavilion offers an
invaluable insight into the various
religious Hindu ceremonies and their
meanings. The textile pavilion has an
extensive collection of traditional
cloth and explains what fabrics are
used when and the significance
behind the symbolism of the
designs. Most exhibits have English
labels. ⏱ *1 hr. Opposite Puputan*

Museum Negri Propinsi Bali, where you can get a good introduction to Balinese culture.

Square. ☎ (0361) 222 680. Admission 6000Rp. Mon–Fri 8am–12.30pm, Sun 8am–3pm.

❷ Pura Jagatnatha. The state temple of Bali is next door to Museum Negri Propinsi Bali and once you've been to the museum, the intricate carvings, symbolic turtles, mythical serpents and various temple statues wrapped in black-and white-checked sarongs (*Polong* cloth) that symbolise good and evil, take on a new meaning. ⏱ *15 min.* See p. 39.

❸ Puputan Square. Opposite the temple and museum is a large park, usually full of kids playing football or flying kites in the afternoon. It was here that the Balinese made a heroic, but ultimately suicidal, stand against the Dutch in 1906. A grand monument commemorates the battle, depicting a Balinese family in heroic pose, complete with jewels in the woman's hand, which according to legend, the women of the Rajah's

court flung at the invaders in order to taunt them. ⏱ *5 min. Corner of Jl Gajah Mada (Dauhpuri Kangin) and Jl Mayor Wisnu.*

A monument commemorating the heroic battle between the Balinese and the Dutch in 1906.

Pasar Badung, Denpasar's main produce market.

offering boxes. The temple dates from the 14th century, and although much of it was damaged in the 1917 earthquake, there are still some very old structures at the back. Look out for the large statues of Garuda. ⏲ *15 min. Admission by donation, but you'll seldom be asked.*

⑦ Puri Pemecutan. Pop into this former palace for a quick look. For a royal residence you might be surprised by its lack of grandeur, but palaces in Bali are relatively plain (compared to temples). It was destroyed in the 1906 invasion, but has since been restored and there are some nice furniture pieces in the main pavilion. ⏲ *5 min. Corner of Jl Mohammad Husni Thamrin (also known as Jl Thamrin) and Jl Hasanudin.*

⑧ Kampung Arab. Jl Hasanudin and Jl Sulawesi are in the heart of the Arabic district of the city, and the streets are lined with gold shops. There's a mosque here, and traffic can get feral before and after prayer times, especially on Fridays. Jl Sulawesi is also great for fabrics. ●

A statue of Catur Muka, the god of four directions.

④ ★★★ Pasar Badung. Denpasar's main produce market is an assault on the senses. The street leading to the entrance is lined with flower sellers and women selling ready-made temple offerings and the air is thick with perfume. Next is a row of food sellers grilling up the delicious *sate lilit* (miniature satay sticks) and other Balinese snacks. Inside the massive three-level market is just about any type of fresh fruit and vegetable and fresh meat (ground level), spice (second level) and food stuff you can imagine. The third level is dedicated to textiles. ⏲ *30 min. Jl Gajah Mada.*

⑤ ★ Pasar Kumbasari. Just across the river from Pasar Badang is the art and craft market, a great place to pick up a souvenir. ⏲ *30 min.* See p. 150.

⑥ Pura Maospahit. You get a real sense of an everyday working temple here, with chickens in cages, men asleep in hammocks and women busily making the little leaf

Beaches **Best Bets**

Jimbaran Beach: golden sand, pounding surf, beautiful sunsets and excellent seafood.

Best **Beachside Promenade**
Sanur *(p. 89)*

Best **Black-Sand Beach**
Candidasa *(p. 88)*

Best **Celebrity Spotting**
Seminyak *(p. 90)*

Best for **Dinner**
Jimbaran *(p. 88)*

Best for **Everything**
Sanur *(p. 89)*

Best for **Families**
Nusa Dua *(p. 89)*

Best for **Getting High (in the Sky)**
Tanjung Benoa *(p. 90)*

Most **Laid-back**
Anturan Beach, Lovina *(p. 88)*

Best for **Learning How to Surf**
Kuta *(p. 89)*

Best for **Massage**
Kuta *(p. 89)*

Best for **Shopping**
Kuta *(p. 89)*

Best for **Sunset**
Kuta *(p. 89)*; and Jimbaran *(p. 88)*

Best **Surf**
Ulu Watu *(p. 90)*

Best for **Water Sports**
Nusa Dua *(p. 89)*

Previous page: Seminyak Beach, the same superb beach as Kuta and Legian, but without the hordes.

The Best Beaches

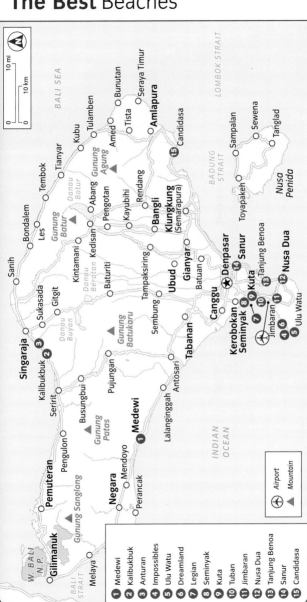

1 Medewi
2 Kalibukbuk
3 Anturan
4 Impossibles
5 Ulu Watu
6 Dreamland
7 Legian
8 Seminyak
9 Kuta
10 Tuban
11 Jimbaran
12 Nusa Dua
13 Tanjung Benoa
14 Sanur
15 Candidasa

Bali Beaches A to Z

The lagoon at Candidasa, a hassle-free place for scenery and swimming.

★★★ **Anturan**   There are no waves to speak of, and the sand is coarse and black, and you'll need to find a space between the brightly painted wooden fishing boats to lay out your towel (no lounges or umbrellas here), and you could quite possibly be pecked to death by one of the many baby chickens that scratch around in the sand, but that's all part of the charm. Anturan has a welcoming at-ease vibe that makes it one of my favourite places to chill out and do nothing, before feasting with the locals on just-caught fish and knocking back a cold Bintang as the sun goes down. *Located 5km west of Singaraja, in the area commonly referred to as Lovina.*

★ **kids Candidasa**   Swaying coconut trees flank this tiny ribbon of black volcanic sand lapped by crystal-clear water. It would have been

perfect once, before the offshore reefs were mined in the 1980s and the sand washed away. Even so, it's a hassle-free place and quite beautiful to look at—and to swim in.

★★★ **Jimbaran**   Golden sand, pounding surf, beautiful resorts, even more beautiful sunsets and a string of seafood restaurants make this one of the most popular beaches in Bali. But, unlike Kuta, it really only gets a crowd at sundown when thousands of people flock here for a seafood dinner. During the day it's easy to find a stretch of deserted sand to call your own. Best swimming is at the southern end, near the Four Seasons Resort.

★★ **Kalibukbuk**   Just like Anturan (see 'Anturan' above) but with a couple of bars that sell seafood and pizza, a beach volleyball court and a

Life's a Beach in Bali

Bali is encircled by beautiful beaches, far too many to cover in this short chapter, so we've just included those with accommodation options that we think are worth using as a base. We know there are many perfect slivers of wave-lapped sand that we haven't mentioned here, but that doesn't mean you shouldn't get out there and seek them out for yourself. Happy hunting!

phallic-looking dolphin monument. The village meeting place is under the tree beside the beach volleyball court, where men sit and smoke while watching over their prize roosters in their bamboo cages, women gossip while making temple offerings and kids kick a football. Most people call it Lovina rather than Kalibukbuk but everyone calls it laid-back. *Located 11km west of Singaraja.*

Kuta   You want a beer? Massage? Sarong? Ice cream? Kite? Chess set? Necklace? Massage? Sarong? Coke? Surf lesson? Massage? You'll want for nothing on Bali's most famous beach, largely because you'll never be left alone long enough. Thousands of people can't be wrong though, it is a beautiful beach and the surf is legendary. Go early in the morning before the crowds arrive and it can be quite deserted, just a few women leaving their daily offerings of flowers and incense in the sand. Come sunset and it can feel as if the whole world has descended on the beach and it takes on a carnival atmosphere. Always swim in the patrolled areas as the surf and strong currents can be tricky.

Nusa Dua, a beach of blinding white sand and cerulean blue water.

Kalibukbuk, a laid-back village meeting place.

★ Legian   It can be hard to tell where Kuta stops and Legian begins, but it's roughly around Jl Melasti, where the road is blocked to traffic and the hawkers become marginally less relentless and the crowds less dense. Like Kuta, most stretches of beach are patrolled, and there are plenty of umbrella-shaded lounges for hire.

★★ kids Nusa Dua   You won't be hassled by hawkers on the beach at Nusa Dua because they've all been locked out of the resort enclave. You also won't find any cheap hotels or beachside *warungs* (food stalls); Nusa Dua is one long strip of four- and five-star beachfront hotels, which can make it feel a little sterile sometimes, but it's great for families and those that just want to spend a few days lying on the beach in peace. And what a beach; blinding white sand and cerulean blue water without any scary waves. The only thing remotely irritating about Nusa Dua is the constant buzz of jet skis and speed boats pulling parasailers and banana boats all day.

★★★ Sanur   Perfect. That's the best way to describe Sanur if you ask me. Edged by one of the most attractive beachside promenades in Bali, it's got brilliant white sand, umbrella-shaped trees for shade,

Bali's Best Breaks

It was the surfers who first discovered Bali, and the often perfect waves still draw them in from all around the world. The best surf is on the southern side of the island: during the dry season (April to September) the southwest is best; during the rest of the year head east.

Ulu Watu is Bali's most famous surfing destination, where huge waves roll in from across the Indian Ocean to crash against perpendicular cliffs, but it's definitely not for beginners. They should head to **Kuta**, **Jimbaran** or **Seminyak**. Experienced surfers will find much to please them just about anywhere on the Bukit Peninsula, including the aptly named **Dreamland** and **Impossibles**. The reefs that protect the beaches at **Nusa Dua** and **Sanur** can be amazing in the right conditions, and **Medewi**, way out west, is famous for its long left-hand wave.

Sanur, as good as it gets.

clean clear water, a few little waves here and there to make it interesting, dozens of great little beachside cafes and bars, and enough local life to remind you that you are indeed in Bali, but none of the aggressive sales pitches you'll get on Kuta and none of the crowds. Yep. Perfect.

★★ Seminyak   It's the same superb beach as Kuta and Legian, but without the hordes. Swim, surf and lie in the sun. It's the best stretch of beach west of the airport. If you're walking from Kuta or Legian, you'll know you're there when you suddenly realise you haven't been asked if you'd like a massage for a while. For those with a map it's just past Jl Arjuna (Jl Double Six).

Tanjung Benoa   The only reason to visit this beach is to hook yourself up to a fast boat in a parasail or some other high-flying or water-skimming device. The beach itself is thin, rocky in places and crowded with boats.

★ kids Tuban   Kuta's southern sister is sleepier, but the sand gets a little narrow in sections. Smaller waves mean it can be good for kids and there are some hotels here that actually front the beach. Officially Tuban Beach stretches west from the airport to Jl Pantai Kuta. ●

Bali's often perfect waves are a big draw-card for surfers.

Adventures on Land

⊕	Airport
☂	Beach
▲	Mountain
〰	Scuba Diving

1 Bungy Jump
2 Horseriding
3 Elephant Trekking
4 Downhill Cycling
5 Treetop Adventure Park

Previous page: Rice paddies are a beautiful feature of Bali's great outdoors.

You don't have to get wet in Bali to enjoy the great outdoors. Whether you want to fly through air on the end of a rope or rubber cord, trek through the jungle on the back of a swaying elephant or race down a mountainside on two spinning wheels, there's a land-based adventure out there for everyone. START: **Double Six Beach, Legian.**

A bungy jump can inject a bit of adrenaline into your relaxing holiday.

❶ ★★ Bungy jump. The uninitiated might think it's a crazy thing to do, but once you've done your first bungy jump you'll be back for more. Do two jumps and you can do your third in style, riding a BMX bike off the platform. Inspired by the manhood ritual on Vanuatu's Pentecost Island, where young men jump from 35m towers with vines tied around their feet, the modern bungy jump using latex rubber cords (with or without the BMX) is the ultimate swan dive. *The bungy tower has long been a landmark opposite Double Six Beach, but is set to move to the beach in front of the Discovery Mall in Tuban by the time you read this.* ☎ *(0361) 731 144. www.ajhackett. com. Jumps from US$99, second jump US$35. AE, MC, V. Daily noon–8pm; Fri & Sat 2am–6am.*

❷ kids Horseriding. There a number of places you can saddle up and ride along the beach or beside rice paddies, and most will pick you up and return you to your Southern Bali hotel. Prices begin at around US$65 for a two-hour ride. I recommend **Umalas Equestrian Resort**. *Jl Lestari 9X, Kerobokan.* ☎ *(0361) 731 402. www.balionhorse.com.*

❸ kids Elephant trekking. There have never been native elephants in Bali, but that doesn't mean you can't ride one through the jungle at a number of theme/safari parks. Your best option is **Bali Safari & Marine Park** or **Elephant Safari Park.** *See p. 29.*

❹ ★★★ Downhill cycling Why go up when going down is so much more fun? Join a downhill cycling tour of winding mountain and village back roads, either from Ubud or from Kintamani at the top of the volcano. Tour prices vary and most tours are a full day. Contact **Bali Bike Baik Tours**. *Banjar Laplapan, Petulu, Ubud.* ☎ *(0361) 978 052. www. balibike.com.*

❺ kids ★ Treetop Adventure Park. Fly through the tree tops with the greatest of ease on a flying fox, flying swing or suspended bridge. There are five adventure circuits, suitable for all ages. It's part of Bedugal Botanic Gardens, which are worth a visit on their own. *Candikuning.* ☎ *(0361) 852 0680. www.bali treetop.com. Admission US$20 adults, US$13 kids.*

View the jungle from the back of an elephant.

Bali on Foot

0	5 mi
0	5 km

▲ *Gunung Penulisan* Tianyar ○

② ▲ ○ Songan

Pura Batur ■ *Gunung Batur* *Danau*
Kintamani ○ ○ Batur *Batur*
Kalanganyar ○ ○ Trunyan
Kedisan ○ ○ Abang ▲ *Gunung Abang*

Danau
Beraten

▲
Gunung
Pohen ○ Baturiti Pengotan ○ *Gunung* ③
Agung ▲

■ **Pura Besakih**
○ Besakih

○ Petang ○ Kayubihi ○ Menanga
○ Muncan
Rendang ○ Sibetan
○ Penebel ○ Melinggih ○ Pulung
Tampaksiring ○ ○ **Bangli** ○ Sidemen
Sembung ○ *Teluk*
Marga ○ *Amuk*
○ Sangeh
Ubud ○ ① ○ Pejeng
Tabanan Mas ○ ○ **Gianyar** **Klungkung**
○ (Semarapura)
○ Mengwi ○ Kusamba ○ ☂ *Kusamba*
○ Kediri ○ Kapal ○ Blahbatu *Beach*
Batuan ○ ☂ *Lebih Beach*
Celuk ○ *BADUNG*
○ Ubung ○ Batubulan ☂ *Ketewel Beach* *STRAIT*
○ **Canggu** ⊛ **Denpasar** ☂ *Padang Galak Beach*
Kerobokan ☂ *Sanur Beach* ⤬ Jungutbatu
Seminyak ○ **Sanur** *Nusa Lembongan* ○ Toyapakeh
Kuta ④ ○ **Legian** *Nusa Ceningan*
Beach ☂ ○ **Kuta** *Pulau Serangan*
Tuban ○ (*Turtle I.*) *Nusa*
NGURAH ○ Tanjung Benoa *Penida*
RAI INT'L ⊕
Jimbaran ○ ☂ *Nusa Dua Beach*

○ **Nusa Dua**

○ Pecatu

☂ *Green Bali Beach*

① Ubud's Rice Paddies and Rivers
② Gunung Batur
③ Gunung Agung
④ Tuban to Seminyak

⊕	Airport
☂	Beach
▲	Mountain
■	Point of Interest
⤬	Scuba Diving

Walking in Bali isn't a wilderness experience. Some of my favourite walks are just off the main street in Ubud into a world of green rice paddies and jungle-clad hills. From village encounters to top-of-the-world sunrise views, you'll see a lot more of Bali if you explore it by foot. START: **Ubud**.

A walk around the outskirts of Ubud can yield some incredible scenery.

1 ★★★ Ubud's rice paddies and rivers. It doesn't really matter in which direction you set off from, it won't take you long in Ubud to find yourself surrounded by terraced rice paddies, raging rivers or dense jungle, or probably all three. A favourite is the loop from north of the town centre along the Campuan Ridge and west to Payogan and back to town. Another good route is through the valley of the Ayung River to Sayan before climbing up through the jungle to hook up with the main road back to Ubud near Kedewatan. You can pick up more-detailed maps of the area from the tourist information centre opposite the Ubud Palace in the town centre. ⏲ *3–4 hr.*

2 ★ Gunung Batur. One of Bali's most popular mountain treks is a nighttime hike to the top of Gunung Batur, Bali's second-highest volcano (1717m), to see the sunrise from the summit. Most trips set off (from your hotel) at around 2am and take about two hours of solid climbing to reach the summit. Guides are

compulsory and you can expect to share your sunrise view with a small crowd of fellow hikers. You'll find information about trekking agencies and guides for climbing both Batur and Agung (see below) at most hotels or tour outlets. ⏲ *7 hr.*

3 ★★ Gunung Agung. You can also watch the sunrise from atop Gunung Agung, Bali's highest and most sacred volcano (see p. 23). The walks are tougher and longer than Batur. Depending on the route you choose it will take between four and seven hours to reach the summit, and while guides aren't compulsory, you'd be mad not to use one, especially if climbing in the dark. ⏲ *9–12 hr.*

4 ★★★ Tuban to Seminyak. Didn't bring your hiking boots to Bali? No problem. The 7km walk along the beach from Tuban to Seminyak is one of the first things I do when I arrive in Bali. Love or hate Kuta, it's still a beautiful beach. ⏲ *2 hr.*

Gunung Agung, Bali's most sacred volcano, is a challenging walk.

Watersports

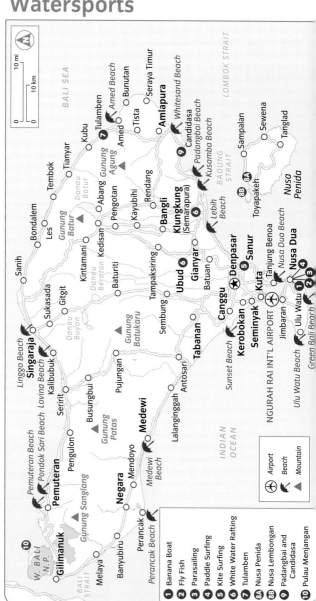

1 Banana Boat
2 Fly Fish
3 Parasailing
4 Paddle Surfing
5 Kite Surfing
6 White Water Rafting
7 Tulamben
8A Nusa Penida
8B Nusa Lembongan
9 Padangbai and Candidasa
10 Pulau Menjangan

Airport
Beach
Mountain

BALI SEA

LOMBOK STRAIT

BADUNG STRAIT

INDIAN OCEAN

BALI STRAIT

W. BALI N.P.

Amed Beach
Bunutan
Seraya Timur
Whitesand Beach
Candidasa
Padangbai Beach
Kusamba Beach
Lebih Beach
Nusa Penida
Sampalan
Sewena
Tanglad
Toyapakeh
Green Bali Beach
Ulu Watu Beach
Nusa Dua Beach
Tanjung Benoa
Jimbaran
Ulu Watu
Nusa Dua
Kuta
Seminyak
Kerobokan
NGURAH RAI INT'L AIRPORT
Canggu
Denpasar
Sanur
Ubud
Gianyar
Batuan
Bangli
Klungkung (Semarapura)
Amlapura
Tulamben
Amed
Tista
Kubu
Tianyar
Tembok
Bondalem
Sanih
Les
Sukasada
Gitgit
Seririt
Singaraja
Kalibubuk
Lovina Beach
Pondok Sari Beach
Pemuteran Beach
Linggo Beach
Pemuteran
Pengulon
Busungbiu
Pujungan
Medewi
Medewi Beach
Lalanginggah
Antosari
Tabanan
Sunset Beach
Sembung
Tampaksiring
Baturiti
Kintamani
Kedisan
Abang
Pengotan
Kayubihi
Rendang
Gunung Agung
Gunung Batur
Danau Batur
Danau Buyan
Danau Beratan
Gunung Batukaru
Gunung Patas
Gunung Sanglang
Mendoyo
Negara
Perancak
Perancak Beach
Melaya
Banyubiru
Gilimanuk

Nusa Penida

10 mi
10 km

A good time in Bali is more often than not a wet time. Be it on the water, over the water, in the water or under the water, there are more ways to have fun getting wet in Bali than just about anywhere else. Water babies should make a base in Nusa Dua or Benoa for motorised sports, Sanur for wind-driven frolics, Ubud or Candidasa for river rafting, and anywhere on the east or north coast for diving that will take your breath away. START: **Nusa Dua or Benoa.**

Banana boating, a watersport everyone can master.

1 **kids** ★★★ **Banana boat.** This is a watersport that everyone can master. All you need to do is hang on tight and try not to swallow too much sea water when you squeal with delight. For those not quite sure what a banana boat is, it's a long plastic tube (shaped a little like a banana) that you sit astride while it's dragged behind a fast boat, and it's lots of fun. Almost every resort at **Nusa Dua** offers banana boat rides. *Expect to pay at least 100 000Rp per 15-minute ride.*

2 **Fly fish.** The concept's the same as a banana boat, but you cling to an inflatable raft-type thing that sails (or more correctly, gets bounced around) through the air as you speed along. Perfect for those who think banana boat rides are for kids. They're most popular at larger resorts in **Nusa Dua** and **Benoa**. *2 or 3 rounds 180 000Rp–250 000Rp.*

3 ★★ **Parasailing.** A tad more sophisticated and smooth than the fly fish, parasailing involves flying aloft in a parachute that's attached to a speeding boat, and getting a thorough dunking in the water at the end. You can hardly see the sky sometimes in Benoa for the canopies in the air, while the harbour is a nightmare of speeding boats looking more at their airborne clients than at the traffic—accidents happen more often than you'd like. I prefer the slightly less crowded skies a little further down the beach at **Nusa Dua**, where your best options are the larger resorts. *Per flight 125 000Rp–150 000Rp.*

4 **Paddle surfing.** The latest on-the-water craze is paddling yourself around (and catching the occasional wave) while standing up on a surf-board. I confess I haven't yet had the chance to try it out, but they tell me it is easier than it looks, and it certainly looks like a lot of fun. Check out **Bali Waterworld** at the Laguna Resort & Spa (p. 110) and the Westin Resort (p. 114), both in Nusa Dua. *3-hour lesson US$55.*

Sail through the air (or get bounced around) as you speed along on a fly fish.

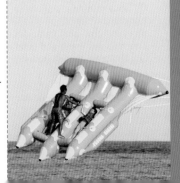

Parasailing is a popular sport; try Nusa Dua for a less crowded experience.

watersport fun that reaches speeds and heights that look and feel jet propelled. Naturally, given that Sanur is the best place in Bali to fly a kite, it's also the best place to learn how to kite surf—or for those that have already mastered the technique, to rent the equipment. Contact **Bali Kitesurfing School**. *Sanur.* ☎ *(0361) 789 9013. www. bali-kitesurfing.org. 2-hour beginner lesson 900 000Rp.*

❻ ★★★ White water rafting.
Bali has two popular white water rafting rivers: the Ayung River, northwest of Ubud, and the Telaga Waja River, north of Klungkung, both offering grade 2 to grade 4 rapids. Best time to go is between October and March, when rapids are at their most exciting. Expect to pay around US$65 to US$80 for a full-day tour. I recommend **Sobek Bali Utama**. ☎ *(0361) 898 7166. www.balisobek.com.* ●

❺ Kite surfing. Combine surfing with kite flying and what do you get, an extreme source of

Underwater Bali

Colourful coral reefs, bountiful marine life and warm clear water combine to make Bali a favourite with divers and snorkellers alike. Top below-the-surface spots include the wreck of the *USS Liberty*, sunk by Japanese in 1942 near **❼ Tulamben** on the far northeast coast; the coral gardens of **❽Ⓐ Nusa Penida** and **❽Ⓑ Nusa Lembongan**, two islands off the east coast; **❾ Padangbai and Candidasa**, the best places to see sharks and other big fish; and **❿ Pulau Menjangan** on the western tip of the island, renowned for its soft coral, tropical fish and sea caves. The reefs off **Sanur** and **Nusa Dua** also offer good snorkelling opportunities, if you don't fancy getting wet but still want to see coral, you can take a trip in a glass bottom boat. You'll find dive shops at all these locations, but always check their credentials before putting your life and lungs in their hands.

The colourful coral reefs in Bali are a drawcard for divers and snorkellers.

Accommodation Best Bets

Perched atop a 350m-high cliff overlooking Jimbaran Bay, the Ayana Resort and Spa has stunning views and luxurious spa treatments.

Best Bathrooms
★★★ Ayana Resort and Spa $$$$$
Jl Karang Mas Sejahtera, Jimbaran
(p. 107)

Best on the Beach
★★★ Conrad Bali $$$$ *Jl Pratama 168, Tanjung Benoa (p. 109)*

Best Garden
★★ Bali Hyatt $$$$ *Jl Danau Tamblingan, Sanur (p. 107)*

Best for Golfers
Amanusa $$$$$ *Jl Nusa Dua Selatan, Nusa Dua (p. 106)*

Best for Kids
Club Med Bali $$$$ *Lot No 6, Nusa Dua (p. 109)*

Best Luxury
★★★ Alila Villas Ulu Watu $$$$$
Jl Belimbing Sari, Banjar Tambiyak, Desa Pecatu (p. 105)

Best for Pampering
★★★ Uma $$$$ *Jl Raya Sanggingan, Banjar Lungsiakan, Kedewatan*
(p. 113)

Best Place to Pretend You're a Local
Space at Bali Villas $$$ *Jl Drupadi 8, Seminyak (p. 113)*

Best Pool
Laguna Resort & Spa $$ *Kawasan Pariwisata Nusa Dua Lot 2, Nusa Dua (p. 110)*

Most Romantic
Amankila $$$$$ *Manggis (p. 106)*

Best Value
★★ Nick's Pension $ *Jl Bisma, Ubud*
(p. 110)

Best Views
★★★ Alila Villas Ulu Watu, $$$$$
Jl Belimbing Sari, Banjar Tambiyak, Desa Pecatu (p. 105)

Previous page: A sublime private pool at Alila Villas Ulu Watu.

Kuta & Legian Accommodation

Legend:
- ⬈ Beach
- ⓘ Information
- ▪ Point of Interest
- 🅿 Police Station
- ✉ Post Office

Jl Padma Uttara

Jalan Legian

Sungai Mati

Jl Pantai Legian

Jl Padma Timur

Jl Padma (Jl Yudistra)

LEGIAN

Jl Batu Pageh

Jl Sriwijaya

Jl Melasti

Jalan Dewi Sri

Jl Patih Jelantik

Legian Beach

Jl Pantai Banjar Pande Mas

Jl Lebak Bene

Jl Pattimura-Kuta

Jl Benesari

Jalan Mangga

Jalan Majapahit

Jl Mataram

Jalan Imam Bonjol

INDIAN OCEAN

Poppies Gang 2 (Jl Batu Bolongo)

Jl Legian

Jl Raya Kuta

Kuta Beach

Poppies Gang 1

Jl Mataram

Jl Majapahit

Jl Raya Kuta

Jl Pantai Kuta

Jl Tegalwangi

🅿 ⓘ

Jl Singosari-Kuta (Jl Bakung Sari)

KUTA

✉

Jalan I Gusti Ngurah Rai

Discovery Mall (Kartika Plaza)

Jalan Kartika Plasa (Jl Dewi Sartika)

Jl Kingkong

Jl Kubu Anyar

Jalan Raya Kuta

Jalan Kek Depos

Jl Samudra

Jl Kubu Anyar

0   1/2 mi

0   0.5 km

All Seasons **2**
Bali Coconut Hotel **1**
Best Western Resort **6**
Hard Rock Hotel **5**
Mercure Kuta Bali **4**
Pullman Bali Legian Nirwana **3**

Bukit Peninsula Accommodation

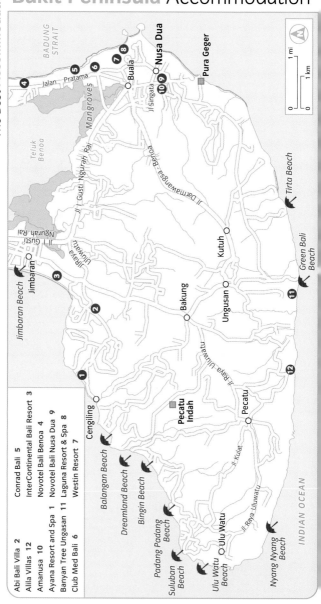

Abi Bali Villa **2**
Alila Villas **12**
Amanusa **10**
Ayana Resort and Spa **1**
Banyan Tree Ungasan **11**
Club Med Bali **6**

Conrad Bali **5**
InterContinental Bali Resort **3**
Novotel Bali Benoa **4**
Novotel Bali Nusa Dua **9**
Laguna Resort & Spa **8**
Westin Resort **7**

Sanur, Lovina & Candidasa
Accommodation

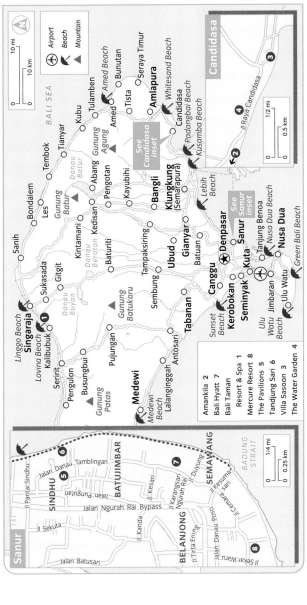

Amankila **2**
Bali Hyatt **7**
Bali Taman
Resort & Spa **1**
Mercure Resort **8**
The Pavilions **5**
Tandjung Sari **6**
Villa Sasoon **3**
The Water Garden **4**

Seminyak Accommodation

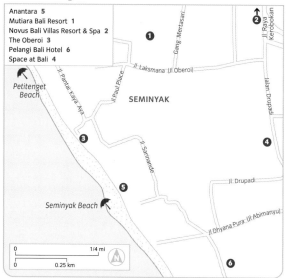

Anantara **5**
Mutiara Bali Resort **1**
Novus Bali Villas Resort & Spa **2**
The Oberoi **3**
Pelangi Bali Hotel **6**
Space at Bali **4**

Jl. Raya Kerobokan

Gang Mertasari

Jl. Laksmana (Jl Oberoi)

Jalan Drupadi

Petitenget Beach

Jl. Pantai Kaja Aya

Jl. Paul Place

SEMINYAK

Jl. Sarmande

Jl. Drupadi

Seminyak Beach

Jl. Dhyana Pura (Jl Abimanyu)

| 0 | 1/4 mi |
| 0 | 0.25 km |

Ubud Accommodation

Jl. Lungsiakan

Jl. Rsi Markandya 3

Sungai Wos

| 0 | 1/2 mi |
| 0 | 0.5 km |

P Police Station
✉ Post Office

Jalan Kedewatan

SANGGINGAN

Jl. Campuan

CAMPUAN

Jl. Kajeng

Jl. Suweta

Jl. Sriwedari

Jl. Sandat

Jalan Raya Andong

UBUD KAJA

Jl. Raya Ubud

Jalan Sayan

KUTUH

Jl. Campuan 1

Jl. Bisma

Monkey Forest Rd
(Jl Wenara Wanu)

Jl. Hanoman

Jl. Sugriwa

Jl. Stukma

UBUD KELOD

Amandari **1**
Kamandalu **3**
Nick's Pension **4**
Novus Taman Bebek
  Resort & Spa **5**
Uma **2**

Bali Accommodation A to Z

Abi Bali Villa JIMBARAN   The pool villas in this brand-new villa complex are lovely, but I'd only stay here if you've booked one of those. The other villas are nice enough, and roomy, but the location is inconvenient: in Jimbaran you either want to be on or near the beach, or at least have a view from the cliff-tops. This place has neither, nor does it have a decent pool for those not lucky enough to have a private one of their own. That said, it does offer a free shuttle service to Jimbaran and a taxi home costs only US$1 or US$2. *Jl Karang Mas Sejahtera 89.* ☎ *(0361) 708 889. www. abibalivilla.com. 28 units. Doubles US$110–US$386. AE, MC, V. Map p. 102.*

★★★ Alila Villas ULU WATU The ultimate in luxury, this all-villa, make that all-pool-villa, resort perched on the edge of a cliff is architecturally stunning. Each villa has ocean views, although with an epic 800 steps down the hill to the beach, you may want to stay right where you are, or just laze by the 50m infinity-edge pool. There's a gym and spa, two restaurants and everything you could possibly want in the villas. You may never want to leave. *Jl Belimbing Sari, Banjar Tambiyak, Desa Pecatu.* ☎ *(0361) 848 2166. www.alilahotels.com/uluwatu/. 84 units. Doubles US$1080–US$1250. AE, MC, V. Map p. 102.*

All Seasons LEGIAN   Bright and cheerful rooms decorated with lots of colour and all mod cons are just one of the reasons to stay here. The others include a great location in the heart of Legian, not too far from the beach, and wallet-friendly rates. *Jl Padma Utara.* ☎ *(0361) 767 688. www.allseasonslegian.com. 113 units. Doubles US$65–US$200. AE, MC, V. Map p. 101.*

Amandari UBUD   The free-standing thatched bungalows are meant to be just like a Balinese village, although I doubt most villagers live in luxury quite like this. Each suite has a garden courtyard and an outdoor bathroom with a sunken tub. Some suites have pools and some have views of the river gorge or surrounding rice paddies, and they all

You may never want to leave Alila Villas, the ultimate in luxury.

A note on prices

Almost all hotels in Bali, apart from the most basic *losmen* (home stays), will quote room prices in US dollars, converting to Indonesian rupiah at the current rate of exchange on the day you check out. To make things easier, in this chapter we've used US dollars, just like the hotels.

have lots of Balinese touches. *Jl Raya Kedewatan.* ☎ *(0361) 975 333. www.amanresorts.com. 30 units. Doubles US$800–US$2150. AE, MC, V. Map p. 104.*

Amankila MANGGIS   Perfect for honeymooners and anyone else wanting lots of peace and quiet in opulent surrounds. This lavish hilltop resort, not far from Candidasa on the east coast, is in the heart of the royal temple district. Suites are on stilts and have fantastic sea views, and there's a buggy to take you down to the beach at the base of the cliff if you don't fancy the five-minute walk. The three-tiered infinity-edge pool is simply stunning. *Manggis.* ☎ *(0363) 41333. www.amanresorts.com. 34*

units. *Doubles US$800–US$1900. AE, MC, V. Map p. 103.*

Amanusa NUSA DUA   Another gorgeously luxe resort by Amanresorts, Amanusa has all the requisite trimmings, such as gym, tennis courts and 30m pool, and rooms with four-poster beds and sunken baths. It's popular with golfers, with one of the best golf courses in Asia separating the resort from the ocean. Non-golfing partners can chill out at the beach or get a massage in their room. Look out for special deals that include complimentary golf. *Jl Nusa Dua Selatan.* ☎ *(0361) 772 333. www.amanresorts.com. 35 units. Doubles US$800–US$1200. AE, MC, V. Map p. 102.*

At Amandari, you get the high-luxury version of a Balinese village.

Amankila, perfect for honeymooners and anyone else wanting peace and quiet in opulent surrounds.

Anantara SEMINYAK   A luxury beachfront hotel with a spa that specialises in rooftop massages, this a great spot to base yourself if you want to be in the heart of the action in Seminyak. Get a room with a balcony for a private viewing of one of the best sunset shows around. *Jl Abimanyu (Dhyana Pura).* ☎ *(0361) 737 773. www.bali.anantara.com. 59 units. Doubles US$550–US$650. AE, MC, V. Map p. 104.*

★★★ Ayana Resort and Spa

JIMBARAN   Perched atop a 350m-high cliff overlooking Jimbaran Bay, the cliff villas are stunning, but then again, the hotel rooms are pretty good, too. There's a choice of four pools—either on the top of the cliff or at the base near the beach— an 18-hole putting course, 12 restaurants, a 40-room spa recently voted the best in the world in *Condé Nast Traveller* magazine and one of the coolest bars—half suspended over the ocean—on the island. *Jl Karang Mas Sejahtera.* ☎ *(0361) 702 222. www.ayanaresort.com. 368 units. Doubles US$210–US$750. AE, MC, V. Map p. 102.*

Bali Coconut Hotel LEGIAN   There's nothing fancy about this older-style hotel, but if you're looking for a basic room with ensuite and air conditioning that works in the centre of Legian, and just happens to be a hop, skip and jump from the beach and won't break the bank, then this is a good choice. *Jl Padma Utara.* ☎ *(0361) 754 122. www.hotelbalicoconut.com. 36 units. Doubles US$40–US$50. MC, V. Map p. 101.*

★★ Bali Hyatt SANUR   This luxe hotel is right on the beach in Sanur, but it's the extensive gardens that set this place apart—they are worth a stroll even if you aren't staying here. The pools aren't bad either. *Jl Danau Tamblingan.* ☎ *(0361) 281 234. www.bali.resort.hyatt.com. 386 units. Doubles US$112–US$230. AE, MC, V. Map p. 103.*

Bali Taman Resort & Spa LOVINA   The rooms are far from luxurious, but they do have air conditioning and a TV, and even the standard rooms have a balcony, and given that they cost just US$30 a

The clifftop pool at Ayana Resort and Spa is a picturesque place to take a dip.

night, you can't expect much more. Opt for a deluxe room and spend most of your time lazing around the pool or wandering along the beach, which the resort fronts. *Jl Raya Lovina.* ☎ *(0362) 41126. www.balitaman.com. 30 units. Doubles US$30–US$45. MC, V. Map p. 103.*

Banyan Tree Ungasan ULU WATU   Banyan Tree always does luxe well, and spas even better, and the new Banyan Tree in Bali is no exception. It's pool villa, clifftop and five star all the way, with some of the best Indian Ocean views in Bali. *Jl Melasti, Banjar Kelod, Ungasan.*

☎ *(0361) 300 7000. www.banyan tree.com. 72 units. Doubles US$535–US$1200. AE, MC, V. Map p. 102.*

Best Western Resort KUTA Tucked away on a back street in the Tuban end of Kuta, this new hotel offers great value with big rooms full of all the mod cons, like marble bathrooms, flat screen TVs and free wi fi, that would cost double the price in any other city in the world. It's a 10-minute walk down tiny laneways to the heart of Kuta and the beach, but sometimes it's nice to be where the locals live, rather than your fellow tourists. *Jl Kubu Anyar 118.* ☎ *(0361) 767 000.*

What's in a name?

Just because a hotel or resort has cottages or beachfront in its name, it doesn't mean that's what you'll get. Some cottage hotels are three-storey hotel complexes, and beachfront may mean you're opposite the beach but there's actually a busy road and a forest of *warungs* (food stalls) to cross before you hit the sand, especially in Kuta.

book.bestwestern.com. *75 units.
Doubles US$45–US$75. AE, MC, V.
Map p. 101.*

kids Club Med Bali NUSA DUA
One price fits all at Club Med,
because everything is included in
the daily rate, even food and most
drinks. A popular choice for families,
there's plenty of sports and activities and facilities, including golf and
a spa, for everyone. Kids under four
stay free and there are three kids
clubs for different ages, so teenagers don't have to mix it with eight
year olds and nursery equipment
for infants. *Lot No 6 Nusa Dua.
☎ (0361) 771 521. www.clubmed.
com.au. 393 units. Doubles from
US$288, although 4 to 7-night pack-
ages are much better value. AE, MC,
V. Map p. 102.*

★★★ Conrad Bali NUSA DUA
The Conrad is one of the best beachfront hotels in Nusa Dua. With several swimming pools, spa, kids club,
water sports, free daily meditation
and workout classes, lots of sched-
uled activities and watersports,
beachside bars and several restaurants, there's no real reason to leave
this place once you're here, although
it's an easy walk to the village of Tanjung Benoa if you do. The Conrad
Suite section of the complex offers
an extra dose of restrained luxury,
with enormous suites, a separate
pool and a lounge that includes complimentary cocktails in the early evening. *Jl Pratama 168, Tanjung Benoa.
☎ (0361) 778 788. www.conrad
hotels.com. 360 units. Doubles
US$215–US$505. AE, MC, V. Map
p. 102.*

Hard Rock Hotel KUTA   Love
your rock and roll? You'll love the
Hard Rock, with its line-up of live
music, it's own recording studio,
and rooms decorated with photos
and memorabilia of various rock
gods and legends. It also has an

incredible free-form pool, a very
good spa and a rock climbing wall. *Jl
Pantai Banjar Pande Mas. ☎ (0361)
761 869. bali.hardrockhotels.net.
418 units. Doubles US$135–US$300.
AE, MC, V. Map p. 101.*

**★★★ InterContinental Bali
Resort** JIMBARAN   The rooms are
elegant, the resort is beachfront
and it's in a great spot in the heart
of Jimbaran. The surf school will
keep teenagers (and adults) happy,
and the kids club is great for under
12s. *Jl Uluwatu 45n. ☎ (0361) 701
888. www.bali.intercontinental.com.
418 units. Doubles US$150–US$530.
AE, MC, V. Map p. 102.*

★★ Kamandalu UBUD   There's
lots of lovely Balinese architectural
touches everywhere you look at this
hillside resort overlooking the terraced rice paddies outside Ubud.
Villas feature four-poster beds and
resort facilities include two pools
(there's a separate one for kids), a
spa and a games room. *Jl Raya
Andong, Banjar Nagi. ☎ (0361) 975
825. www.kamandaluresort.com. 54
units. Doubles US$210–US$540. AE,
MC, V. Map p. 104.*

*Club Med Bali is a popular choice
for families.*

Laguna Resort & Spa is beachfront, but also has a man-made swimming lagoon that meanders through the hotel's landscaped gardens.

Laguna Resort & Spa NUSA DUA   This hotel is beachfront, but it also offers more than 5000 sq. m of lagoon (Bali hotel speak for free-form pool with man-made sandy beaches) swimming space that meanders through the hotel's land-scaped gardens. *Kawasan Pariwi-sata Nusa Dua Lot 2.* ☎ *(0361) 771 327. www.starwoodhotels.com. 271 units. Doubles US$190–US$300. AE, MC, V. Map p. 102.*

★ Mercure Kuta Bali KUTA   The rooms are a bit on the small side, but are bright and cheery and some have great ocean views from the balcony. The hotel's in a great location in the middle of Kuta. *Jl Pantai Kuta 10X.* ☎ *(0361) 767 411. www.mercurekutabali.com. 130 units. Doubles US$120–US$350. AE, MC, V. Map p. 101.*

Mercure Resort SANUR   Set right on the beach in sleepy Sanur, this hotel is a good midrange budget choice, with two pools, kids club, spa and free shuttle bus to the local shopping area. The family rooms, which include a separate children's

area, are popular with families. *Jl Mertasari, Sanur.* ☎ *(0361) 288 833. www.mercureresortsanur.com. 189 units. Doubles US$120–US$175. AE, MC, V. Map p. 103.*

Mutiara Bali Resort SEMINYAK   A good midrange choice if you want to stay in the heart of Seminyak but don't want to spend up big on the superluxe beachfront resorts. It's only a couple of minutes' walk to the best eating street in Seminyak and a few minutes more to the beach. Room are spacious, bathrooms border on huge and there is a nice pool. *Jl Braban 88 Br. Taman Seminyak.* ☎ *(0361) 734 966. www.mutiara bali.com. 46 units. Doubles US$115–US$165. AE, MC, V. Map p. 104.*

★★ Nick's Pension UBUD   For a cheapie, the rooms are pretty good. They're simple and lack amenities such as a TV, but some have air con-ditioning. There's a serviceable pool, and it's in a good location in the heart of Ubud. Some rooms overlook the river; others a small rice paddy, and it's very quiet. Wake up in the morning to a thermos of tea on your porch and an incense-wafting offering to the gods left at your front step. *Jl Bisma.* ☎ *(0361) 975 636. www.nickshotels-ubud. com. 24 units. Doubles US$27– US$65. MC, V. Map p. 104.*

Novotel Bali Benoa TANJUNG BENOA   Balinese-style rooms surrounded by lush gardens and with easy access to the beach make this a good midrange budget choice, with a range of activities from morning aerobics to puppet making and Balinese dance lessons. *Jl Pratama.* ☎ *(0361) 772 239. www.novotel balibenoa.com. 180 units. Doubles US$100–US$200. AE, MC, V. Map p. 102.*

Novotel Bali Nusa Dua NUSA DUA   The pool at this resort inside the gated community of Nusa Dua is a whopping 1500-sq. m. It's beachfront is flanked by an 18-hole golf course, and it has a spa and a free kids club, so the whole family is kept happy. *Jl Pantai Mengiat, BTDC Complex.* ☎ *(0361) 848 0555. www. novotelnusaduabali.com. 175 units.*

Novus Bali Villas Resort & Spa: very beautiful, very stylish, very Balinese.

Nick's Pension, a quiet, affordable option in the heart of Ubud.

Doubles US$100–US$160. AE, MC, V. Map p. 102.

★★ Novus Bali Villas Resort & Spa SEMINYAK   Very beautiful, very stylish, very Balinese is the best way to describe this all-villa property in northern Seminyak, surrounded by rice paddies and peace and quiet. Perfect for honeymooners. *Jl Pengubugan, Banjar Silayukti, Kerobokan.* ☎ *(0361) 411 388. www. novushotels.com. 20 units. Doubles US$250–US$650. AE, MC, V. Map p. 104.*

★★★ Novus Taman Bebek Resort & Spa UBUD   Overlooking the Ayung River, this boutique resort has some of the best views in Ubud. Fans of Colin McPhee's seminal book about living in Bali (*A House in Bali;* see p. 164 Savvy Traveller/Books on Bali) will be interested to note that the resort is built on the land that he once lived on. Each villa is designed after a different period and culture, ranging from French Colonial to Malay and Australian Queenslander. There's a pool and spa, but no restaurant or

Stay at Novus Taman Bebek Resort & Spa for some of the best views in Ubud.

bar—only room service. It's the perfect place to escape the world and write a great novel. *Jl Raya Sayan, Br. Kutuh, Sayan.* ☎ *(0361) 975 385. www.novushotels.com. 11 units. Doubles US$125–US$700. AE, MC, V. Map p. 104.*

★★★ **The Oberoi** SEMINYAK If you want to splash out on a bit of luxury, this is a good place to do it. Near the southern tip of Seminyak Beach, each villa, furnished with teak and Balinese art, has its own high coral-wall courtyard garden, providing a wonderful sense of privacy and seclusion. Beyond the meticulously groomed stretch of beach the resort features beautiful gardens, a spa, gym and pool. *Jl Kayu Aya, Seminyak Beach.* ☎ *(0361) 730 361. www.oberoi hotels.com/oberoi_bali/. 75 units. Doubles US$320–US$800. AE, MC, V. Map p. 104.*

★★★ **The Pavilions** SANUR Most hotels offer you a welcome drink on arrival, at the Pavilions you also get a welcome foot massage, very welcome indeed after a long

flight. Located on the main street of Sanur, a long tunnel-like driveway of bamboo delivers you into a world of peace and tranquillity. The free-standing, very private villas, some two-storey, some with private plunge pool, at this beautiful boutique property are all spacious and elegantly decorated. Sanur's relaxed and shady beach is only a five-minute walk away. *Jl Danau Tamblingan 76.* ☎ *(0361) 288 381. www.thepavilionsresorts.com. 23 units. Doubles US$165–US$440. AE, MC, V. Map p. 103.*

Pelangi Bali Hotel SEMINYAK Good-value rooms on the beach in Seminyak can be hard to find, but the Pelangi delivers. Rooms, all with balconies, are well sized but bathrooms are a bit poky. The restaurant is a great place to watch the sun go down. *Jl Dhyana Pura.* ☎ *(0361) 730 346. www.pelangibali.com. 89 units. Doubles US$90–US$120. MC, V. Map p. 104.*

Pullman Bali Legian Nirwana LEGIAN It looks and feels a bit like a business hotel you could find anywhere, but this brand-new option in the centre of the Kuta-Legian region only opened at the time of writing, so you know everything is new and fresh. *Jl Melasti 1.* ☎ *(0361) 762 500. www.pullman hotels.com. 351 units. Doubles US$115–US$230. AE, MC, V. Map p. 101.*

Space at Bali SEMINYAK The next best thing to having your own house in Bali is renting a private villa for a week or two. There are six two-bedroom villas at Space, and each one comes with its own private butler and chef service, pool and garden, and pretty much anything else you need to make yourself at home. Rates indicated are per villa, so despite the luxury, it's not as expensive as it looks. *Jl Drupadi 8.* ☎ *(0361) 731 100. www. spaceatbali.com. 6 units. Doubles US$350–US$550. AE, MC, V. Map p. 104.*

★★ **Tandjung Sari** SANUR This lovely boutique hotel on the beach at Sanur has been welcoming guests since 1962. Back then it was just a four-bungalow extension of the family home. Now there are 26 bungalows surrounded by lush gardens and decorated with Balinese art and antiques. *Jl Danau Tamblingan 29.* ☎ *(0361) 288 441. www. thepavilionsresorts.com. 26 units. Doubles US$230–US$335. MC, V. Map p. 103.*

★★★ **Uma** UBUD Open-air bathrooms, peaceful valley views and gorgeous tropical gardens makes the Uma a delightfully peaceful retreat, just a 20-minute walk from bustling Ubud. If you need extra help relaxing, try an early morning yoga class in the open-air yoga pavilion or spend some time in the meditation bale, reflexology area or 25m jade-green pool at COMO Shambhala Retreat, also part of the

One of the six two-bedroom villas at Space at Bali, each with its own private pool, butler and chef service.

The Water Garden features pretty little freestanding bungalows set in lush gardens.

resort. *Jl Raya Sanggingan, Banjar Lungsiakan, Kedewatan.* ☎ *(0361) 972 448. www.uma.como.bz. 29 units. Doubles US$260–US$525. AE, MC, V. Map p. 104.*

Villa Sasoon CANDIDASA Stylish villas with beach access, although with your own private pool, you may decide it's better to stay in than brave the hot black sand. Check internet specials for package deals of three nights or more that include activities like free yoga classes, hill treks and massages, which work out much cheaper than the published rate below. *Jl Puri Bagus.* ☎ *(0363) 41511. www.villasasoon.com. 4 units. 1-bedroom villa US$250. AE, MC, V. Map p. 103.*

★ **The Water Garden** CANDI-DASA Pretty little freestanding bun-galows set in lush gardens. It's not beachfront, but each bungalow has a deck overlooking its own fish pond complete with orange and white carp and waterlilies. Rooms are nice enough and feature big four-poster beds romantically festooned with netting, but have no TV. *Jl Raya Candidasa.* ☎ *(0363) 41540. www. watergardenhotel.com. 12 units. Doubles US$100–US$175. AE, MC, V. Map p. 103.*

Westin Resort NUSA DUA All rooms have a private balcony with a view of the free-form pool, tropical gar-dens or beach. It's a popular family choice, with family rooms, free kids club and lots of family-friendly activities, such as Balinese dancing lessons, kite flying, Indonesian lessons and movie nights. *Kawasan Pariwisata Nusa Dua Lot 36.* ☎ *(0361) 771 906. www.starwoodhotels.com. 342 units. Doubles US$160–US$280. AE, MC, V. Map p. 102.* ●

The Best Dining

Dining **Best Bets**

Sate lilit, *a popular Balinese snack.*

Best **on the Beach**
Beach Cafe *Jl Pantai Sindhu,
Sanur (p. 123)*

Best **Cheap Eat**
★★★ Warung Nikmat *Jl Singosari,
Kuta (p. 136)*

Best **Chicken**
★★★ Ayam Taliwanga *Jl Kubu
Anyar, Kuta (p. 123)*

Best **Crispy Duck**
★★★ Bebek Bengil *Jl Hanoman,
Ubud (p. 123)*

Best **Indonesian**
★★★ Bumbu Bali *Jl Pratama,
Tanjung Benoa (p. 125)*

Are you brave enough to eat lawar, *the
extremely spicy and quintessentially
Balinese dish?*

Most **Romantic**
★★ Toke *Jl Raya Candidasa,
Candidasa (p. 134)*

Best **Satay**
★★★ Murni's Warung *Jl Raya
Campuan, Ubud (p. 131)*

Best **Seafood**
★★★ Dewi Sri *Jl Kartika Plaza,
Tuban (p. 127)*

Best **Seafood on the Beach**
★ Teba Cafe *Jl Four Seasons Resort,
Muaya Beach, Jimbaran (p. 134)*

Best Cheap **Seafood on
the Beach**
★ Warung Bamboo *On the beach
east of Jl Kubu Gembong, Lovina
(p. 135)*

Best **Splurge**
★★★ Mozaic *Jl Raya Sanggingan,
Ubud (p. 131)*

Best **Suckling Pig**
★★★ Warung Ibu Oka *Jl Suweta,
Ubud (p. 135)*

Best **View**
★★ La Lucciola *Jl Pantai Kaya Aya,
Seminyak (p. 130)*

*Previous page: Food from Sarong, the
place to see and be seen.*

Kuta & Legian Dining

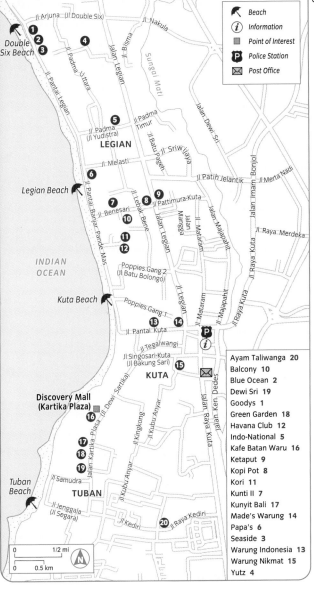

Ayam Taliwanga **20**
Balcony **10**
Blue Ocean **2**
Dewi Sri **19**
Goodys **1**
Green Garden **18**
Havana Club **12**
Indo-National **5**
Kafe Batan Waru **16**
Ketaput **9**
Kopi Pot **8**
Kori **11**
Kunti II **7**
Kunyit Bali **17**
Made's Warung **14**
Papa's **6**
Seaside **3**
Warung Indonesia **13**
Warung Nikmat **15**
Yutz **4**

Seminyak Dining

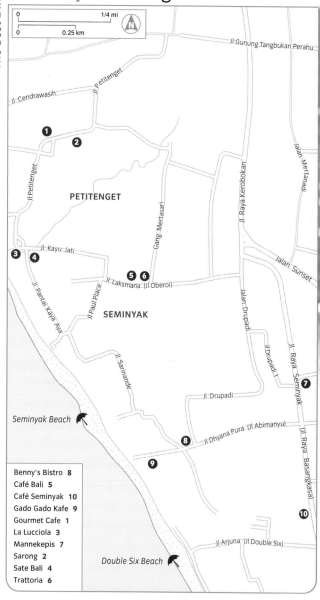

Benny's Bistro **8**
Café Bali **5**
Café Seminyak **10**
Gado Gado Kafe **9**
Gourmet Cafe **1**
La Lucciola **3**
Mannekepis **7**
Sarong **2**
Sate Bali **4**
Trattoria **6**

Seminyak Beach

Double Six Beach

PETITENGET

SEMINYAK

Jl. Gunung Tangbukan Perahu

Jl. Cendrawasih

Jl. Petitenget

Jl. Petitenget

Jl. Kayu Jati

Jl. Pantai Kaya Aya

Jl. Paul Place

Jl. Laksmana (Jl. Oberoi)

Gang. Mertasari

Jl. Raya Kerobokan

Jalan. Mertanadi

Jalan. Sunset

Jalan. Drupadi

Jl. Sarmande

Jl. Drupadi 1

Jl. Drupadi

Jl. Dhyana Pura (Jl. Abimanyu)

Jl. Raya Seminyak

Jl. Raya Basangkasa

Jl. Arjuna (Jl. Double Six)

0   1/4 mi
0   0.25 km

Bukit Peninsula Dining

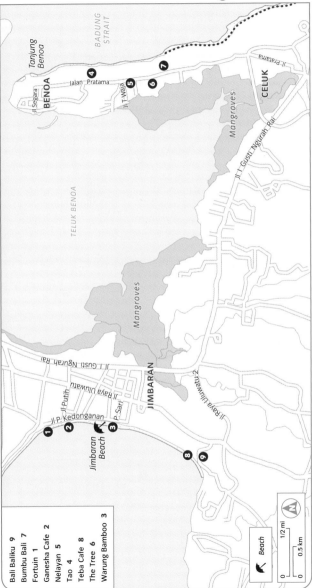

Bali Baliku **9**
Bumbu Bali **7**
Fortuin **1**
Ganesha Cafe **2**
Nelayan **5**
Tao **4**
Teba Cafe **8**
The Tree **6**
Warung Bamboo **3**

Sanur Dining

Anjani **4**
Beach Cafe **2**
Bonsai **3**
Café Batu Jumbar **6**
Casa Luna **7**
Charming **10**
Coriander **8**
Mango Beach Bar **1**
Ming Le Resto **12**
Sanur Beach Market
  Restaurant **5**
Sari Bundo **9**
Stiff Chilli **11**

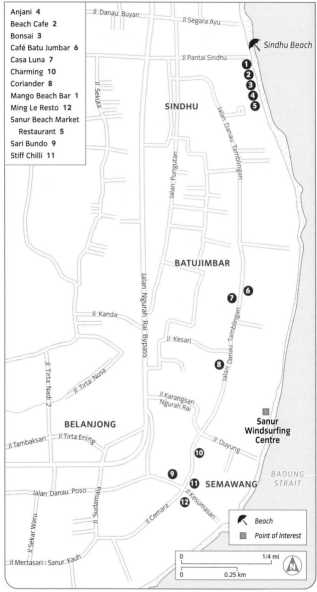

Candidasa Dining

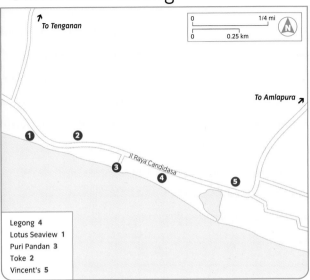

To Tenganan

To Amlapura

Jl Raya Candidasa

0   1/4 mi
0   0.25 km

Legong **4**
Lotus Seaview **1**
Puri Pandan **3**
Toke **2**
Vincent's **5**

Lovina Dining

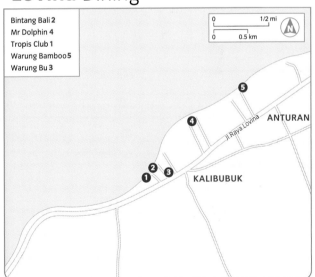

Bintang Bali **2**
Mr Dolphin **4**
Tropis Club **1**
Warung Bamboo **5**
Warung Bu **3**

0   1/2 mi
0   0.5 km

Jl Raya Lovina   ANTURAN

KALIBUBUK

Ubud Dining

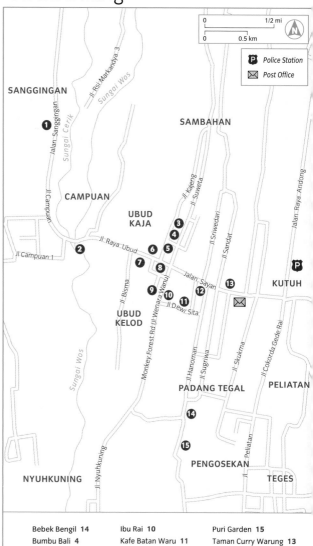

Bebek Bengil **14**

Bumbu Bali **4**

Café Lotus **6**

Casa Luna **7**

Coco Bistro **8**

Ibu Rai **10**

Kafe Batan Waru **11**

Mozaic **1**

Murni's Warung **2**

Nomad **12**

Puri Garden **15**

Taman Curry Warung **13**

Terazo **3**

Tropical **9**

Warung Ibu Oka **5**

Bali Dining A to Z

Anjani SANUR *INDONESIAN/GER-MAN/WESTERN* This tiny restaurant in a cute little garden opposite the beach is just the place to kick back with a tropical fruit juice. It also serves passable pizza. *Jl Danau Tamblingan 31 Sindhu.* ☎ *(0361) 805 0404. Mains 40 000Rp–65 000Rp. No credit cards. Lunch & dinner daily. Map p. 120.*

★★★ **Ayam Taliwanga** KUTA *INDONESIAN* This little restaurant tucked away on a back road at the southern end of Kuta, several blocks inland from the beach, specialises in traditional dishes from Lombok. The mouthwatering *betau ayam*, (grilled chicken smothered in a sauce of garlic, ginger, chilli, lemongrass and a host of other secret Balinese spices) is to die for. Most of the menu is designed to share between two, so you can bank on halving the price indicated below if you bring a friend. *Jl Kubu Anyar.* ☎ *(0361) 800 2000. Mains 25 000Rp–58 000Rp. No credit cards. Lunch & dinner daily. Map p. 117.*

Balcony KUTA *WESTERN/INDONE-SIAN* As popular for breakfast as lunch and dinner, the upstairs room gives prime street viewing below. It has all the usual offerings of *nasi goreng* (fried rice), satays, pasta and so on, but best bets are the seafood skewers or the steaks. *Jl Benesari.* ☎ *(0361) 757 409. Mains 29 000Rp–59 000Rp. No credit cards. Lunch & dinner daily. Map p. 117.*

Bali Baliku JIMBARAN *WESTERN* One of the only restaurants close to (but not on) the beach in Jimbaran that offers anything decent besides fish: meat eaters will be pleased to hear it serves reasonable steak, as well as pasta and chicken. *Jl Bukit*

Crackers and sambals, a tasty snack.

Permai 5A. ☎ *(0361) 708 400. Mains 25 000Rp–120 000Rp. AE, MC, V. Lunch & dinner daily. Map p. 119.*

Beach Cafe SANUR *INDONESIAN/WESTERN* More stylish than most of the beachfront cafes, with comfy wicker sofas and cushions on the sand. Good salads and seafood, as well as Indonesian classics. *Jl Pantai Sindhu.* ☎ *(0361) 282 875. Mains 69 000Rp–82 000Rp. No credit cards. Lunch & dinner daily. Map p. 120.*

★★★ **Bebek Bengil** UBUD *INDO-NESIAN* The name means Dirty Duck, but the duck here is anything but. Famous for its crispy duck, some say it's the best in Bali. If you want the special smoked duck, wrapped in betel leaf, you'll need to order 24 hours in advance. People travel from the south just to eat here in one of the lovely garden cabanas, so bookings are essential. *Jl Hanoman.* ☎ *(0361) 975 489. Mains 44 000Rp–85 000Rp. AE, MC, V. Lunch & dinner daily. Map p. 122.*

Benny's Bistro SEMINYAK *INDO-NESIAN/WESTERN/SEAFOOD* The big outdoor beer garden is perfect for a Bintang or two after a day on the beach. The grilled seafood is good value. *Jl Dhyana Pura (Jl Abimanyu).* ☎ *(0361) 738 587. Mains 39000Rp–99000Rp. MC, V. Lunch & dinner daily. Map p. 118.*

Bintang Bali LOVINA *INDONE-SIAN* Fronting the beach at Kalibukbuk this breezy spot is great for a cold beer (who'd have guessed with a name like that?) or simple Balinese fare. *Jl Ketapang.* ☎ *(0362) 702 1112. Mains 22000Rp–70000Rp. No credit cards. Lunch & dinner daily. Map p. 121.*

Blue Ocean LEGIAN *WESTERN/INDONESIAN* Opened in 1969, Blue Ocean was one of the original cafes catering to Westerners. Back then it was in the middle of nowhere, now it's in the heart of the Double Six eating strip opposite the beach. Great spot for a late breakfast or cold drink—the 'Thirst Lesser' (a refreshing mix that's three parts carrot juice and one part lemon) is just what you need on a hot day. It serves all the usual staples, but seafood's its thing. *Jl Arjuna (Jl Double Six).* ☎ *(0361) 747 2308. Mains 30000Rp–135000Rp. No credit cards. Breakfast, lunch & dinner daily. Map p. 117.*

Bonsai SANUR *INDO-NESIAN/WEST-ERN* Enter from Jl Danau Tamblingan and you'll walk though a large bonsai garden— the garden that is, not the trees, they're all teeny tiny. Enter from the beachfront walk and you won't even know they're there. One of my favourite beachside cafes in Sanur, you can eat inside the pavilion or at tables on the sand. *Jl Danau Tamblingan 27.* ☎ *(0361) 282 909. Mains 44000Rp–114000Rp. MC, V. Breakfast, lunch & dinner daily. Map p. 120.*

Refreshing fresh juices are sure to perk you up on a hot afternoon.

Bumbu Bali in Tanjung Benoa near Nusa Dua is famous for its cooking classes.

Enjoy the open-air pavilion overlooking a gorgeous lotus lily pond at Café Lotus.

★★★ **Bumbu Bali** TANJUNG BENOA *INDONESIAN* If you're looking for excellent Indonesian dishes prepared with flair in a gorgeous setting, head to Bambu Bali. The *rijsttafel (literally, rice table)*, which gives you a taste of just about everything the kitchen does best, is great value at around 185000Rp, or 325000Rp if you choose the seafood option. Chef Heinz von Holden is a well-known cookbook author and his food shows his passion for the cuisine. If you love the food, you can always join one of his cooking classes (see p. 48). *Jl Pratama.* ☎ *(0361) 774 502. Mains 75000Rp–117000Rp. MC, V. Lunch & dinner daily. Map p. 119.*

★ **Bumbu Bali** UBUD *INDONESIAN/INDIAN* Not to be confused with the restaurant of the same name in Nusa Dua, but great Indonesian food nonetheless. Like the Nusa Dua eatery, this Bumbu Bali also runs a regular cooking school (see p. 19, bullet ⑨). *Jl Suweta 1.* ☎ *(0361) 974 217. Mains 35000Rp–69000Rp. MC, V. Breakfast, lunch & dinner daily. Map p. 122.*

★ **Café Bali** SEMINYAK *ASIAN/WESTERN* The décor is very neo-Colonial, with whitewashed wooden furniture and plantation shutters, and swirling overhead fans and amazing light installations by a local lighting artist. The plastic white lace tablecloths let it down, however. The menu is a mix of Western and Southeast Asian dishes, with a good dessert menu. *Jl Laksmana (Jl Oberoi).* ☎ *(0361) 736 484. Mains 38000Rp–85000Rp. MC, V. Lunch & dinner daily. Map p. 118.*

Café Batu Jumbar SANUR *INDONESIAN/WESTERN* Upscale cafe with large deck perfect for people watching in the middle of the main street of Sanur. It's a great spot for ice cream and smoothies, and the very tasty Indonesian and Western classics make it a popular spot with expats and visitors alike. *Jl Danau Tamblingan 75A.* ☎ *(0361) 287 374. Mains 45000Rp–125000Rp. AE, MC, V. Lunch & dinner daily. Map p. 120.*

★★ **Café Lotus** UBUD *INDONESIAN/WESTERN* The beautiful setting is reason enough to eat here. It's right next door to Pura Taman Saraswati and the open-air pavilion overlooks a gorgeous lotus lily pond. Traditional Balinese performances are staged every evening, except Wednesdays and Fridays, and cost 80000Rp (see p. 37) *Jl Raya Ubud.* ☎ *(0361) 975 660. Mains 35000Rp–99000Rp. MC, V. Breakfast, lunch & dinner daily (closed on major Balinese holy days). Map p. 122.*

Café Seminyak SEMINYAK *INDO-NESIAN/WESTERN* Classic cheap eat, but it's the oversized burgers that draw the crowds to this busy little cafe on the border between Legian and Seminyak. *Jl Raya Seminyak 17.* ☎ *(0361) 736 967. Mains 25 000Rp–45 000Rp. No credit cards. Lunch & dinner daily. Map p. 118.*

Casa Luna SANUR *INDONESIAN/CHINESE/WESTERN* Fronting busy Jl Danau Tamblingan, this long narrow open-air pavilion is quite charming. The extensive menu has a range of Chinese dishes as well as the usual Western and Indonesian offerings. *Jl Danau Tamblingan 186.* ☎ *(0361) 288 263. Mains 50 000Rp–85 000Rp. No credit cards. Lunch & dinner daily. Map p. 120.*

Casa Luna UBUD *INDONESIAN/WESTERN* Janet de Neefe, the woman behind the Ubud Writers & Readers Festival (see p. 163) is also the woman behind this popular cafe, which also has a cooking school attached. It's the place to go for fresh pastries and cake, as well as good Indonesian dishes. You can pick up a copy of her book, *Fragrant Rice*, here. It originally started out as a cook book but morphed into a personal story of her love affair with Balinese food and culture. *Jl Raya Ubud.* ☎ *(0361) 977 409. Mains 40 000Rp–90 000Rp. AE, MC, V. Lunch & dinner daily. Map p. 122.*

Charming SANUR *FRENCH* Fine French dining in a gorgeous open-air pavilion featuring lots of carved wood, most of it reclaimed from old boats and local houses. Focus is on seafood and grills, and while a tad more expensive than its neighbours, it's great value given the quality of the food and the classy setting. It's the sister restaurant of one of Sanur's other great restaurants, Ming Le Resto (see p. 131). *Jl Danau Tamblingan 97.* ☎ *(0361) 288 029. Mains 55 000Rp–195 000Rp. AE, MC, V. Lunch & dinner daily. Map p. 120.*

Coco Bistro UBUD *INDONESIAN/THAI/WESTERN* Smart little restaurant near the Ubud Palace with a good choice of Indonesian, Thai and Western dishes. Eat inside or outside closer to the street under hanging lanterns at night. It gets very busy before 7.30pm, when everyone

Casa Luna, a charming restaurant with an extensive menu, including a range of Chinese and Western dishes to complement the Indonesian offerings.

Charming: fine French dining in a gorgeous open-air pavilion.

heads off to a cultural performance across the street, so it pays to book. *Jl Raya Ubud.* ☎ *(0361) 977 000. Mains 29 000Rp–129 000Rp. AE, MC, V. Lunch & dinner daily. Map p. 122.*

Coriander SANUR *INDONESIAN/ THAI/WESTERN* The garlic prawns are reason enough to eat at this clean and tidy little upscale eatery, although the special Thai dishes are also worth trying. The seafood is brought in fresh daily. *Jl Danau Tamblingan 188.* ☎ *(0361) 283 920. Mains 30 000Rp–85 000Rp. MC, V. Lunch & dinner daily. Map p. 120.*

★★★ Dewi Sri TUBAN *SEAFOOD/ CHINESE* It's in a cavernous white room with tiled walls and floors that feels a bit like eating in an empty swimming pool, but the seafood is some of the best I've had in Bali, and at very reasonable prices given the quality. Choose your fish fresh from the tanks that line the wall out the front and order it steamed. While you wait, get a serve of the crab and asparagus soup, a prawn stick or two and some crumbed squid, and be ready to enjoy a feast fit for a couple of kings. Downstairs is nonsmoking, a rarity in Bali. *Jl Kartika Plaza.* ☎ *(0361) 753 737. Mains 40 000Rp–275 000Rp. AE, MC, V. Lunch & dinner daily. Map p. 117.*

Fortuin JIMBARAN *SEAFOOD* One of the better beachside *warungs* close to the fish market at Jimbaran. Like all of these seafood *warungs*, the price is determined by the weight of your fish and is often negotiable. Although it's open for lunch, it's usually empty until around sunset. *Jl Pantai Kedonganan.* ☎ *(0361) 702 553. Mains 80 000Rp– 180 000Rp. No credit cards. Lunch & dinner daily. Map p. 119.*

Gado Gado Kafe SEMINYAK *WESTERN* Despite the name, most of the fare in this beachside restaurant is Western. It's expensive, but you're paying for the million dollar view. It's a great place for sunset drinks (cocktails are 85 000Rp to 105 000Rp) and there's a 50 000Rp three-course kids' menu. *Jl Dhyana Pura 99.* ☎ *(0361) 736 966. Mains 140 000Rp–300 000Rp. AE, MC, V. Lunch & dinner daily. Map p. 118.*

Ganesha Cafe JIMBARAN *SEAFOOD* This little seaside *warung* is spotlessly clean and staff will pick you up from your hotel if you are staying in the local area and deliver you back home again, for free, although you can be sure it's included somewhere within the price of your meal. It also has a good range of cocktails to toast the

Kori, an oasis of calm style.

sunset with. *Jl Pantai Kedonganan.* ☎ *(0361) 858 5222. Mains 70 000Rp–245 000Rp. MC, V. Lunch & dinner daily. Map p. 119.*

Goodys LEGIAN *ITALIAN* Cheap and cheerful pasta beside the sea. Sometimes that's all you really want. It's part of the popular eat street that fronts Double Six Beach. *Jl Arjuna.* ☎ *(0361) 888 4532. Mains 34 000Rp–70 000Rp. No credit cards. Lunch & dinner daily. Map p. 117.*

Gourmet Cafe SEMINYAK *WESTERN* Join the crowds of expats who flock here for their daily caffeine fix and a late breakfast of melt-in-the-mouth pastries. *Jl Petitenget 77A.* ☎ *(0361) 847 5115. Mains 35 000Rp–108 000Rp. MC, V. Breakfast, lunch and early dinner daily. Map p. 118.*

Green Garden TUBAN *INDONESIAN/WESTERN* Family-friendly food, like pasta, pizza, steak and seafood, that appeals to fussy eaters who don't want too much spice with their *nasi goreng*. The satays, cooked over a charcoal grill at the entrance to the restaurant, are pretty good. Staff are young and cheerful, the ambience is relaxed

and it even has high chairs for kids. *Jl Kartika Plaza.* ☎ *(0361) 754 571. Mains 31 000Rp–95 000Rp. AE, MC, V. Lunch & dinner daily. Map p. 117.*

Havana Club KUTA *SPANISH* There's a few Indonesian and Western classics on the menu, but the better choice is the Mexican/Spanish fare. Even if you don't want to eat it's a pleasant place to while away an hour or so over a jug of sangria as you watch the circus that is Kuta pass by. *Poppies Lane I.* ☎ *(0361) 762 448. Mains 37 000Rp–88 000Rp. AE, MC, V. Lunch & dinner daily. Map p. 117.*

★ **Ibu Rai** UBUD *INDONESIAN/WESTERN* This pretty little restaurant sparkles at night when the hanging red-lace covered paper lanterns are lit inside the thatched pavilion. The dishes, both Western and Indonesian, are presented with flair. *Monkey Forest Rd (Jl Wenara Wana).* ☎ *(0361) 973 472. Mains 42 000Rp–75 000Rp. MC, V. Lunch & dinner daily. Map p. 122.*

Indo-National LEGIAN *WESTERN/INDONESIAN* Just like the name implies, this roomy bar and restaurant in the heart of Legian offers a range of Indonesian and Western dishes, and a reasonable selection of Aussie wines. If you're wondering what to do with all those sarongs you've bought, take your cue from here, they make great tablecloths. *Jl Padma 17.* ☎ *(0361) 759 883. Mains 30 000Rp–80 000Rp. No credit cards. Lunch & dinner daily. Map p. 117.*

★★★ **Kafe Batan Waru** KUTA & UBUD *INDONESIAN/WESTERN* Creative Indonesian dishes as well as Western favourites, with a kids' menu and lots of vegetarian options. It's all good, but whatever you do, make sure you try the *tum ayam*, two small parcels of boneless chicken mixed with Balinese spices and young papaya and steamed in banana leaf. They might appear small, but they pack a big flavour punch. There's another location in Ubud (Jl Dewi Sita. ☎ (0361) 977 528, Map p. 122). Jl Kartika Plaza, Kuta. ☎ (0361) 766 303. Mains 26000Rp–105000Rp. AE, MC, V. Lunch & dinner daily. Map p. 117.

Ketaput KUTA SEAFOOD/INDONESIAN Hidden behind a store off busy Jl Legian in the midst of the raucous bars and clubs, Ketaput is much classier than its neighbours. The pretty wooden pavilion, with teak furniture and white linen tablecloths, overlooks a very inviting pool and is quite romantic in the evening. Jl Legian. ☎ (0361) 754 209. Mains 36000Rp–90000Rp. AE, MC, V. Lunch & dinner daily. Map p. 117.

Kopi Pot KUTA CAFE If you need a break from shopping or the noise, traffic and haggling of busy Jl Legian gets you frazzled, retreat into the shady garden of this little cafe for a great selection of coffee and cake. It also serves a good breakfast and there's free wi-fi. Jl Legian. ☎ (0361) 752 614. Mains 25000Rp–80000Rp. No credit cards. Breakfast, lunch & dinner daily. Map p. 117.

Kori KUTA INDONESIAN/WESTERN A cut above all the other eateries along frenetic Poppies Gang II, Kori, with its elegant tables and lovely garden courtyard setting, is an oasis of calm style. Seafood and grills are the speciality, although there's also a range of other Western-style dishes and it serves good cocktails. The place to go when you're sick of cheap and cheerful and want something a little bit more grown-up. Poppies Gang II. ☎ (0361) 758 605. Mains 65000Rp–125000Rp. AE, MC, V. Lunch & dinner daily. Map p. 117.

Kunti II KUTA JAPANESE Primarily a sushi bar, Kunti also offers the usual Japanese classics. Best value, however, is the sushi and sashimi sets for less than 100000Rp. It's tiny, but much more atmospheric than the majority of Japanese restaurants in and around Kuta. Jl Benesari 27. ☎ (0361) 765 148. Mains 30000Rp–100000Rp. AE, MC, V. Lunch & dinner daily. Map p. 117.

★★★ Kunyit Bali TUBAN INDONESIAN The candlelit garden setting and breezy open-walled thatched-roof pavilion are both as entrancing as the food, which is all Balinese and very, very good. House specials, like the Nasi Bali (a mixed platter of rice with minced fish skewers, beef satay, shredded chicken, sticky sweet dried beef and red hot sambal) are hard to beat. Jl Kartika Plaza (next door to Hotel Santika Beach). ☎ (0361) 759 991. Mains

Satay served with lawar, a potent flavour combination!

Sate asem *on the grill.*

38000Rp–115000Rp. AE, MC, V.
Lunch & dinner daily. Map p. 117.

★★ **La Lucciola** SEMINYAK
WESTERN On the beach opposite
Pura Petitenget, with perfect water
views. It's pricey, but most places in
Seminyak with views like this are.
Even if you don't eat here, come for
a sunset drink— the lychee and lime
vodka granitas go down a treat. The
upstairs section is a Balinese rarity,
nonsmoking! *Jl Pantai Kaya Aya.*
☎ *(0361) 730 838. Mains 110000Rp–
245000Rp. AE, MC, V. Brunch, lunch
& dinner daily. Map p. 118.*

Legong CANDIDASA *INDONESIAN/
WESTERN* Cheerful little family-run
eatery decorated with bamboo
temple offerings. It has good-value
three-course set menus for 50000Rp
to 60000Rp, a four-hour happy hour
from 4pm to 8pm, and a free, if a little half-hearted, traditional *legong*
dance show most nights at 7.30pm.
Jl Raya Candidasa. ☎ *(0363) 41052.
Mains 35000Rp–70000Rp. MC, V.
Lunch & dinner daily. Map p. 121.*

★★ **Lotus Seaview** CANDIDASA
ITALIAN/SEAFOOD This breezy
restaurant at the western end of the
Candidasa main road lives up to its
name— it has one of the best sea
views in town. The focus is on fresh
seafood straight off the fishing
boats below, but there's usually a
barbecue most nights. It's a good
place to try suckling pig if you can't

make it to Ubud, or you got a taste
for it while you were there. *Jl Raya
Candidasa.* ☎ *(0363) 41257. Mains
40000Rp–134000Rp. MC, V. Lunch &
dinner daily. Map p. 121.*

★★★ **Made's Warung** KUTA
INDONESIAN More like a restaurant than a traditional *warung*,
Made's has been a popular spot for
tourists since tourists first started
coming to Kutu. It's always busy,
but with good reason. The food,
particularly the *sate lilit* (miniature
beef satay sticks) and *gado gado*
(mixed vegetables with spicy peanut
sauce), is good, there's plenty of
Western dishes for those that crave
food from home and the room is a
pleasant place to escape the hubbub of the surrounding streets.
Jl Pantai Kuta. ☎ *(0361) 755 297.
Mains 25000Rp–75000Rp. AE, MC,
V. Lunch & dinner daily. Map p. 117.*

Mango Beach Bar SANUR *INDO-
NESIAN/WESTERN* Sit back and
soak up the views from the cute
candy-striped lounges on the sand
at this laid-back beachside bar and
restaurant. There's live music most
nights. *Jl Pantai Sindhu.* ☎ *081 138
7211. Mains 28000Rp–90000Rp. No
credit cards. Lunch & dinner daily.
Map p. 120.*

★★ **Mannekepis** SEMINYAK
EUROPEAN This lively little Belgian
bistro does a great *steak frites
(steak with fries)*, and good wraps

and salads for lunch. Thursday, Friday and Saturday nights feature live jazz from 9pm. And look up while you're there, there are fish swimming in a tank on the ceiling. *Jl Raya Seminyak 2.* ☎ *(0361) 847 5784. Mains 40000Rp–120000Rp. MC, V. Lunch & dinner daily. Map p. 118.*

Ming Le Resto SANUR *FRENCH* Very smart and very good. Dress up and treat yourself to some fabulous French fare at this upmarket restaurant set in a lovely garden at the southern end of Sanur's main street. It's expensive by local standards, but you get what you pay for. The best place in Sanur to go for a very special night out. *Jl Danau Tamblingan 105.* ☎ *(0361) 281 948. Mains 45000Rp–355000Rp. AE, MC, V. Lunch & dinner daily. Map p. 120.*

★★★ Mozaic UBUD *FRENCH* Ubud's finest restaurant serves up exquisite French food with small Indonesian twists. Whether you eat in the garden or inside the richly decorated pavilion, you're in for a very memorable meal. *Jl Raya Sanggingan.* ☎ *(0361) 975 768. Set 6-course menus 550000Rp–850000Rp. AE, MC, V. Dinner daily. Map p. 122.*

Mr Dolphin LOVINA *INDONESIAN/ SEAFOOD* The seafood's straight off the boat and its location is a great spot to sit and watch the villagers go about their day. It fronts the patch of shady sand that doubles as a village square outside the temple, around halfway between Lovina and Anturan. *Jl Pantai Banyualit.* ☎ *0813 5327 6985. Mains 15000Rp–60000Rp. No credit cards. Lunch & dinner daily. Map p. 121.*

★★★ Murni's Warung UBUD *INDONESIAN/WESTERN* The four-level restaurant overlooks the river, but it's not just the view that's the drawcard here, the food is terrific. The second level down has a lounge perfect for cocktails while taking in the lush view. *Jl Raya Campuan.* ☎ *(0361) 975 233. Mains 27000Rp–79000Rp. MC, V. Breakfast, lunch & dinner daily. Map p. 122.*

Nelayan TANJUNG BENOA *SEAFOOD/WESTERN* Finding a moderately priced place to eat in and around Nusa Dua can be tricky, as most restaurants are either attached to resorts or cater for the well heeled, but you'll find good-value seafood and Western standards in this little eatery in a thatched pavilion set back from the street. *Jl Pratama 101.* ☎ *(0361) 776 868. Mains 25000Rp–120000Rp. No credit cards. Lunch & dinner daily. Map p. 119.*

Pull up a chair at a beachside restaurant in Sanur for a lazy afternoon.

Mozaic, Ubud's finest restaurant: the place to go for a memorable meal.

★★★ Nomad UBUD *INDONESIAN/ WESTERN* At first glance Indonesian tapas might not make much sense, but the little tasting plates are a great way to browse the best of the Indonesian menu. Start with three for 29 000Rp or work your way up to the full set of 12 for 90 000Rp. All the vegetables are organic. *Jl Raya Ubud 35.* ☎ *(0361) 977 169. Mains 35 000Rp–70 000Rp. AE, MC, V. Lunch & dinner daily. Map p. 122.*

Papa's LEGIAN *ITALIAN/CAFE* A great place to go if you need to escape the sun and surf for an ice-cold freshly squeezed juice or a good Italian coffee. It's alfresco and right opposite the beach, but don't expect a view—all you can see is the beach wall and busy Kuta beach road. It also serves good sandwiches for a light lunch (55 000Rp to 65 000Rp) home-made pasta and wood-fired pizza. *Jl Pantai Kuta.* ☎ *(0361) 755 055. Mains 69 000Rp– 179 000Rp. AE, MC, V. Lunch & dinner daily. Map p. 117.*

Puri Garden UBUD *INDONESIAN/ WESTERN* If you're hankering after a decent coffee in Ubud, this is a good choice— you can even get

Kopi Luwak, the famous 'cat poo' coffee here, although at 60 000Rp for a small cup, it's double what you pay at the plantations nearby (see p. 48, bullet ⑤). It also has a great selection of exotic juice blends. I haven't been game to try the bean, cabbage, apple and guava blend (good for digestion, apparently), but remain hopeful for the lettuce, plum, apple and carrot punch, which promises to make you more beautiful, and prevent split ends. *Jl Pengosekan.* ☎ *(0361) 973 310. Mains 26 000Rp–60 000Rp. MC, V. Lunch & dinner daily. Map p. 122.*

Puri Pandan CANDIDASA *INDO-NESIAN/SEAFOOD* From the street it looks like just another hotel (it is) but tucked away down the back is a cheap little beach-front restaurant with million dollar views. The seafood is particularly good value. *Jl Raya Candidasa 14.* ☎ *(0363) 41541. Mains 30 000Rp– 75 000Rp. MC, V. Lunch & dinner daily. Map p. 121.*

Sanur Beach Market Restaurant SANUR *INDONESIAN/WESTERN* Standard Western and Indonesian

Bali's famous coffee made from Kopi Luwak.

dishes served beachside, but what makes this breezy bar and restaurant different from its neighbours is that your beer and burger or *nasi goreng* is all for a good cause. All profits go to the Sanur Village Foundation and are used to build schools, art centres, dispensaries and temples. *Jl Segara Ayu.* ☎ *(0361) 288 574. Mains 39 000Rp–125 000Rp. No credit cards. Lunch & dinner daily. Map p. 120.*

Sari Bundo SANUR *INDONESIAN* Eat with the locals at this spotlessly clean Padang restaurant in southern Sanur. Pick what you want from the window display and pay (not very much) by the dish. Chicken's its thing, and it's all good, but beware, most of it is fiery hot. *Jl Danau Poso.* ☎ *(0361) 281 389. Mains 5000Rp– 12 000Rp. No credit cards. Breakfast, lunch & dinner daily. Map p. 120.*

Sarong SEMINYAK *WESTERN/ FUSION* This dark and moody baroque eatery festooned with black chandeliers and gold organza is the latest place to see and be seen in Seminyak. Go just for drinks or go for dinner, but you'll need to book, and dress up. *Jl Petitenget 19X.* ☎ *(0361) 737 809. Mains 88 000Rp–159 000Rp. AE, MC, V. Dinner daily. Map p. 118.*

★★★ **Sate Bali** SEMINYAK *INDO-NESIAN* Good Indonesian food can be hard to find in Seminyak, where most of the eateries tend towards Western and European, but Sate Bali is a stand out. Go for one of the three *rijsttafels* with a selection of eight classic Balinese dishes. You can learn how to make them yourself in a morning Balinese cooking class. *Jl Laksmana 22A (Jl Oberoi).* ☎ *(0361) 736 734. Mains 49 000Rp– 85 000Rp, or 165 000Rp for rijsttafel. No credit cards. Lunch & dinner daily. Map p. 118.*

Seaside LEGIAN *WESTERN/MEXI-CAN* More stylish than most of the eateries along Double Six Beach, the two curved terraces offer prime sunset viewing, especially if you can nab a seat on the second level. The menu includes a good range of burgers and sandwiches for lunch, and once the sun goes down, lots of fish and steak as well as pizza and Tex-Mex. *Jl Arjuna.* ☎ *(0361) 737 140. Mains 35 000Rp–150 000Rp. AE, MC, V. Lunch & dinner daily. Map p. 117.*

Stiff Chilli SANUR *ITALIAN* Pop into this little corner cafe at the southern end of Sanur beach for a good coffee or a gelato and take in the beach views. Despite the name, the menu also features a good range of pizza and pasta. *Jl Kesumasari 11.* ☎ *(0361) 288 371. Mains 30 000Rp– 68 000Rp. MC, V. Breakfast, lunch & dinner daily. Map p. 120.*

Taman Curry Warung UBUD *INDONESIAN/WESTERN* A good-value eating house with an art gallery attached, although the food is better than the art. Cheap and cheerful, with good Indonesian classics. *Jl Raya Ubud.* ☎ *(0361) 975 633. Mains 23 000Rp–33 000Rp. No credit cards. Lunch & dinner daily. Map p. 122.*

Sarong, a dark and moody baroque eatery.

Tum bebek, a Balinese dish at Sate Bali, a standout for good Indonesian food in Seminyak.

Tao TANJUNG BENOA *THAI/WESTERN* Sit back and watch the paragliders sail by at this upmarket beachside cafe. Housed in a charming open-air wooden pavilion, the prices are on the high side, but the food is good. It's a nice spot for a light lunch, or something more substantial once the sun goes down. *Jl Pratama 96.* ☎ *(0361) 772 902. Mains 38 000Rp–100 000Rp. AE, MC, V. Lunch & dinner daily. Map p. 119.*

★ Teba Cafe JIMBARAN *SEAFOOD* This busy beachside eatery is in the most southern of the three Jimbaran seafood *warung* strips, and one of the better ones. It's a good option for lunch, even better for dinner, although if entering from the beach side it's hard to tell where one cafe starts and the next begins. Drinks are almost double the daytime price once the sun sets, but the atmosphere is magic. *Jl Four Seasons Resort, Muaya Beach.* ☎ *(0361) 703 156. Mains 35 000Rp–175 000Rp. MC, V. Lunch & dinner daily. Map p. 119.*

Terazo UBUD *INDONESIAN* This stylish bar and restaurant decorated with vintage travel posters is a welcome change from the ubiquitous thatched pavilion. The food, too, best described as Balinese 'fusion', makes a nice change from the standard offerings. Great wine list and cocktails. *Jl Suweta.* ☎ *(0361) 978 941. Mains 49 000Rp–175 000Rp. AE, MC, V. Lunch & dinner daily. Map p. 122.*

The Tree TANJUNG BENOA *INDONESIAN/WESTERN* More of a pub than a restaurant, although the meals aren't bad, this place has a large leafy beer garden, which can be just the place to hide away on a hot day. *Jl Pratama.* ☎ *(0361) 773 488. Mains 39 000Rp–118 000Rp. MC, V. Lunch & dinner daily. Map p. 119.*

★★ Toke CANDIDASA *WESTERN/INDIAN/MEXICAN* One for the romantics! Candlelit garden cabanas festooned with organza curtains make this a great spot for a special dinner *au deux*. The menu is also sure to appeal, with something to please everyone, from Indonesian and Western classics to Mexican and Indian dishes. *Jl Raya Candidasa.* ☎ *(0363) 41991. Mains 40 000Rp–85 000Rp. MC, V. Lunch & dinner daily. Map p. 121.*

Trattoria SEMINYAK *ITALIAN* The service is haphazard and a bit off-hand, but the home-made pasta is good, as is the pizza, and the prices are good. There are two branches on the same street, around 100m apart. The northern one is not so poky. *Jl Laksmana (Jl Oberoi).* ☎ *(0361) 746 0253. Mains 44 000Rp–91 000Rp. AE, MC, V. Lunch & dinner daily. Map p. 118.*

Tropical UBUD *WESTERN* This busy little cafe in the heart of central Ubud serves a smattering of good Indonesian classics, including a great satay, seafood, pasta and grills. *Monkey Forest Rd 3 (Jl Wenara Wana).* ☎ *(0361) 971 122. Mains 32 000Rp–125 000Rp. AE, MC, V. Lunch & dinner daily. Map p. 122.*

Tropis Club LOVINA *INDONESIAN/ WESTERN* Watch the beach volley-ball action (if there is any) with a freshly blended juice or ice-cream sundae. Once the sun goes down there's wood-fired pizza and acoustic music most nights. *Jl Ketapang.* ☎ *(0362) 42090. Mains 20 000Rp–90 000Rp. No credit cards. Breakfast, lunch & dinner daily. Map p. 121.*

Vincent's CANDIDASA *WESTERN* Enjoy a cocktail in the wicker lounges out the front while listening

Beachside tables

to jazz, then eat in the garden court-yard out the back, which, when can-dlelit at night, is quite romantic. *Jl Raya Candidasa.* ☎ *(0363) 41368. Mains 45 000Rp–120 000Rp. MC, V. Lunch & dinner daily. Map p. 121.*

Warung Bamboo JIMBARAN *SEAFOOD* The seafood *warungs* in the middle section of the Jimbaran Beach strip, in among the fishing boats, are a much more low key affair than their northern neigh-bours, who often cater for bus groups. But, like all the others, tables are right at the water's edge, particularly during high tide when the waves can lap at your feet, and the seafood is fresh, and marginally cheaper than the more formal eater-ies to the north and south. *Jl Pantai Kedonganan.* ☎ *(0361) 702 1888. Mains 60 000Rp–150 000Rp. No credit cards. Lunch & dinner daily. Map p. 119.*

★ Warung Bamboo LOVINA *INDONESIAN* Sit back and watch the fishermen tend their boats and nets while tucking into cheap-as-chips fresh fish grilled in a banana leaf, and try not to accidentally kick the chickens scratching around your feet at this tiny little *warung* on the sand at Anturan Beach, just east of Lovina. *On the beach east of Jl Kubu Gembong.* ☎ *No phone. Mains 15 000Rp–30 000Rp. No credit cards. Lunch & dinner daily. Map p. 121.*

Warung Bu LOVINA *INDONE-SIAN* Dirt cheap home-cooked food makes this little *warung* on Lovina's busy main road a winner. *Jl Raya Lovina.* ☎ *(0362) 41928. Mains 13 000Rp–15 000Rp. No credit cards. Lunch & dinner daily. Map p. 121.*

★★★ Warung Ibu Oka UBUD *INDONESIAN* Be prepared to line up for some of the best *babi guling* (suckling pig) in Bali. If there are no

Toke, a place for the romantics!

or satay. *Off Poppies Gang II.*
☎ *(0361) 759 817. Mains 10 000Rp–*
30 000Rp. No credit cards. Lunch &
dinner daily. Map p. 117.

★★★ Warung Nikmat KUTA

INDONESIAN The dishes are displayed behind a glass counter and
you pick and choose what you want
and pay according to how many
dishes you order, with prices ranging from 1000Rp to 5500Rp for
more expensive items such as
chicken. It's all good and a few dollars will buy you more than you can
eat. It's popular with locals and
expats, so get there early because
all the best bits will be gobbled up
by midafternoon. *Jl Singosari*
☎ *(0361) 764 678. Mains 10 000Rp–*
25 000Rp. No credit cards. Until
around 7pm daily. Map p. 117.

tables free, and there probably
won't be, you can get takeaway.
Just order the *'spesial'*. *Jl Suweta.*
☎ *(0361) 976 345. Mains 25 000Rp–*
40 000Rp. No credit cards. 11am–
7pm daily. Map p. 122.

Warung Indonesia KUTA *INDO-*
NESIAN Cheap and cheerful, you
can fill your belly here for just US$1
or US$2. It also has a few Western
dishes, like pizza and burgers, but
better choices are the *nasi goreng*

Yutz LEGIAN *EUROPEAN* If you're
hankering for some bratwurst or
schnitzel, this is the place to go, it
has a wide selection of sausages
and other German and Austrian
dishes, as well as a smattering of
Indonesian classics and the ever-
popular burger and grills. *Jl Pura*
Bagus Taruna 52. ☎ *(0361) 765 047.*
Mains 35 000Rp–95 000Rp. No credit
cards. Breakfast, lunch & dinner
daily. Map p. 117. ●

Why not top off a day of lounging on the beach with some fresh calamari?

Shopping **Best Bets**

Silk umbrellas make great souvenirs.

Best **Balinese Designer Fashion**
★★★ Paul Ropp *Jl Raya Seminyak 39, Seminyak (p. 146)*

Best **Baskets**
★★ Dari Bali *Jl Hanoman 23, Ubud (p. 145)*

Best **Bikinis**
★★★ Blue Glue *Jl Raya Bansangkasa 6, Seminyak (p. 145)*

Best **Books**
★★ Periplus *Discovery Mall, Jl Kartika Plaza, Tuban (p. 146); and Monkey Forest Rd, Ubud (p. 146)*

Best **Feel Good Buy**
sks *Jl Laksmana 40 (Jl Oberoi), Seminyak (p. 146)*

Best **Handwoven Fabrics**
★★★ Threads of Life *Jl Kajeng 24, Ubud (p. 147)*

Best **Kites**
★ Flying Dragon *Jl Raya Ubud, Ubud (p. 150)*

Best **Local Market**
★★ Pasar Ubud *Jl Raya Ubud, Ubud (p. 149)*

Best **Puppets**
★★★ Wayan's Shop *Jl Raya Ubud, Ubud (p. 145)*

Best Cheap **Sarongs**
Pasar Sari Meta Nadi *Jl Melasti, Legian (p. 149)*

Best **Souvenirs**
★★★ Pasar Kumbasari *Jl Gajah Mada, Denpasar (p. 150)*

Best **Silk Umbrellas**
★★ Wibisana *Jl Raya Basangkasa 7, Seminyak (p. 148)*

Handwoven baskets in Ubud. Previous page: A colourful array of temple baskets for sale at a Kuta market.

Kuta & Legian Shopping

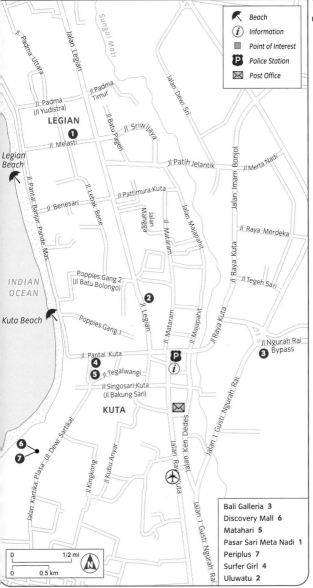

Legend:
- 🏖️ Beach
- ℹ️ Information
- ⬜ Point of Interest
- 👮 Police Station
- ✉️ Post Office

Jl Padma Uttara
Jalan Legian
Sungai Mati
Jl Padma Timur
Jalan Dewi Sri
Jl Padma (Jl Yudistra)
LEGIAN ❶
Jl Batu Pageh
Jl Sriw Jaya
Jl Melasti
Legian Beach
Jl Patih Jelantik
Jl Merta Nadi
Jalan Imam Bonjol
Jl Pantai-Banjar-Pande Mas
Jl Lebak-Bene
Jl Benesari
Jl Pattimura-Kuta
Jalan Mangga
Jl Mataram
Jalan Majapahit
Jl Raya Merdeka
Jl Raya Kuta
INDIAN OCEAN
Poppies Gang 2 (Jl Batu Bolongo)
❷
Jl Tegeh Sari
Kuta Beach
Poppies Gang 1
Jl Legian
Jl Mataram
Jl Majapahit
Jl Raya Kuta
Jl Ngurah Rai Bypass ❸
Jl Pantai Kuta
❹
Jl Tegalwangi
❺
Jl Singosari-Kuta (Jl Bakung Sari)
KUTA
Jalan Ken Dedes
Jalan I Gusti Ngurah Rai
❻
Jl Kartika Plasa (Jl Dewi Sartika)
❼
Jl Kingkong
Jl Kubu Anyar
Jalan Raya Kuta
Jalan I Gusti Ngurah Rai

0   1/2 mi
0   0.5 km
N

Bali Galleria **3**
Discovery Mall **6**
Matahari **5**
Pasar Sari Meta Nadi **1**
Periplus **7**
Surfer Girl **4**
Uluwatu **2**

Seminyak Shopping

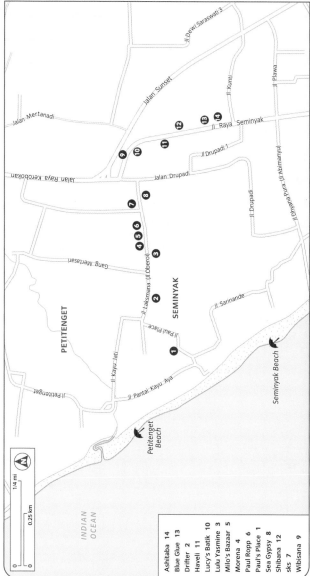

Ashitaba **14**
Blue Glue **13**
Drifter **2**
Haveli **11**
Lucy's Batik **10**
Lulu Yasmine **3**
Milo's Bazaar **5**
Morena **4**
Paul Ropp **6**
Paul's Place **1**
Sea Gypsy **8**
Shibana **12**
sks **7**
Wibisana **9**

Ubud Shopping

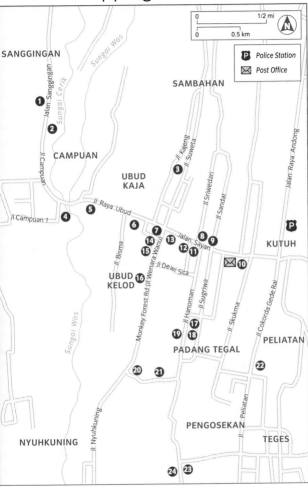

0		1/2 mi
0	0.5 km	

P Police Station
✉ Post Office

SANGGINGAN

Sungai Wos

Sungai Cerik

Jalan Sanggingan

SAMBAHAN

Jl Campuan

CAMPUAN

Jl Campuan 1

UBUD KAJA

Jl. Kajeng

Jl. Suweta

Jl. Raya Ubud

Jl. Sriwedari

Jl. Sandat

Jalan Raya Andong

KUTUH

Jl. Bisma

Jalan Sayan

Monkey Forest Rd (Jl Wenara Wana)

Jl. Dewi Sita

UBUD KELOD

Sungai Wos

Jl. Hanoman

Jl. Sugriwa

Jl. Stukma

Jl. Cokorda Gede Rai

PELIATAN

PADANG TEGAL

NYUHKUNING

Jl. Nyuhkuning

PENGOSEKAN

Peliatan

TEGES

Agung Rai **22**	Macan Tiger **15**	Sei-Sui **1**
Dari Bali **19**	Maha Blanco Jewellery **4**	Studio Perak **11**
Dolphin Family **20**	Mangku Made Gina **23**	Tanda Mata **7**
Flying Dragon **6**	Moari **9**	Tegun Folk Art Gallery **17**
Gajah Mas Gallery **24**	Pasar Ubud **13**	The Yoga Shop **18**
Ganesha Bookshop **10**	Periplus **14**	Threads of Life **3**
Harmonis **16**	Pondok Bamboo Music Shop **21**	Toko East **12**
Kupu Kupu Gallery **8**	Rai Sandi **2**	Wayan's Shop **5**

Around the Island & Denpasar Shopping

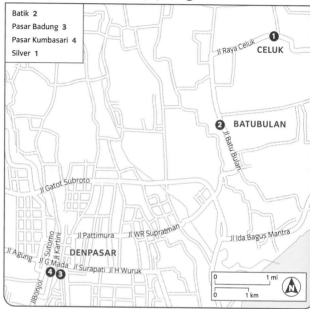

Batik **2**
Pasar Badung **3**
Pasar Kumbasari **4**
Silver **1**

Jl Raya Celuk   **1** CELUK

2 BATUBULAN

Jl Batu Bulan

Jl Gatot Subroto

Jl Pattimura   Jl WR Supratman   Jl Ida Bagus Mantra

Jl Agung   Jl Sutomo   Jl Kartini   Jl G Mada   **DENPASAR**

Jl Bonjol   **4** **3** Jl Surapati   Jl H Wuruk

0 _____ 1 mi
0 _____ 1 km

Bali Shopping A to Z

Art & Handicrafts
★★ Agung Rai UBUD   This co-operative of artists is a good place to buy fine art, because the money goes directly back to the artists themselves. The full range of Balinese painting styles is represented in several showrooms built around an inner courtyard, and woodwork and batik are featured as well, also available for purchase. *Jl Peliatan.* ☎ *(0361) 975 449. AE, MC, V. Map p. 141.*

Batik BATUBULAN   Batulbulan, on the road to Ubud, is one of the centres for batik production and there

are dozens of showrooms in the area. Almost every tour will stop at a batik factory and showroom, where you can watch the process and then buy from the usually huge selection of sarongs, shirts and other clothing, as well as home-wares and 'art' pieces to frame and hang on your wall. These are usually better quality, using natural dyes, than the stuff you'll find around Kuta and other urban centres. Always check the back, real batik should appear on both sides, unlike screen-printed fabric. A good one to visit, although very popular with tour

Wares for sale at Dolphin Family, a cute little shop opposite the Monkey Forest.

buses, is **Sari Amerta** (☎ (0361) 299 057; AE, MC, V). Some of it is tacky, some of it is very nice, it all depends on your taste. *Batubulan, Gianyar. Map p. 142.*

Dolphin Family UBUD   Who'd of thought that so many things could be encrusted with multicolour plastic beads and still look good? This cute little shop opposite the Monkey Forest sells everything from jewellery, hair clips, shoes, handbags, baskets and clothing. All covered in thousands of beads, of course. It makes to order if you have your own beaded fantasy just begging to come alive. *Monkey Forest Rd (Jl Wenara Wana).* ☎ *(0361) 974 430. No credit cards. Map p. 141.*

Watch the ancient craft of hand-dying decorative fabrics at a batik factory near Batubulan on the road to Ubud.

Gajah Mas Gallery UBUD   An exhaustive selection of very high-quality Balinese fine art, running the full gamut of style from traditional to contemporary over two large floors. If you're serious about taking home a piece of fine art, this is a good place to go. *Jl Raya Pengosekan.* ☎ *(0361) 976 283. AE, MC, V. Map p. 141.*

Kupu Kupu Gallery UBUD   The range of handicrafts is modest, but shopping here will definitely make you feel good. All the items are made by local people with disabilities, and in a country with no health care or social security, spending your money here is helping these artists support themselves. *Jl Raya Ubud (opposite Jl Hanoman).* ☎ *0812 362 8720. No credit cards. Map p. 141.*

★★★ **Macan Tiger** UBUD Quality indigenous arts and antiques from all over Indonesia are beautifully displayed in this large store that has six rooms full of tribal art, carvings, sculpture, fabrics, baskets, jewellery and brass bowls. Everything's fixed price, so you can give your haggling skills a rest. *Monkey Forest Rd (Jl Wenara Wana).* ☎ *(0361) 977 121. AE, MC, V. Map p. 141.*

★ **Mangku Made Gina** UBUD   Beautiful handwoven baskets are the drawcard at this unassuming shop in Pengosekan village.

A basketweaver at work.

The owner also paints and has a range of traditional art, but it's the intricate baskets that steal the show. *Jl Raya Pengosekan.* ☎ *(0361) 975 725. MC, V. Map p. 141.*

Uluwatu KUTA There are 10 Uluwatu boutiques scattered around Kuta, Legian, Seminyak, Sanur, Ubud and Nusa Dua, but this one's the largest and has the biggest collection of beautiful handmade lace that originates in Tabanan in Western Bali. The range is exclusively black or white, and limited to simple but elegant linen and cotton clothing and tablecloths. They make great souvenirs. *Jl Legian.* ☎ *(0361) 751 933. AE, D, MC, V. Map p. 139.*

Bargaining

Everything's negotiable in Bali, even hotels rates are open to discussion in the low season, and shops will often offer you a 20 per cent discount off the marked price as soon as you walk in the door. The trick to bargaining is not to take it too seriously. Always smile and keep your good humour—after all it's a bit of a game. And remember that the final 1000Rp you are negotiating over is worth less than US$0.15—so does it really matter? Always have a rough idea in your head of how much you want to pay, and once you agree on a price you are committed to buying. As a guide, start at around a third of the asking price and it's expected that you make two or three counter offers. If you can't agree, walk away—if the price was fair, the vendor will probably call you back, if not, then you know your offer was too low.

★★★ Wayan's Shop UBUD

Beautiful puppets and intriguing wooden masks are the highlights in this shop. The masks are decorated with batik designs that have been painted in the traditional way with hot wax, directly onto the wood and then dried in the sun. The shop next door is Wayan's, too, and has even more puppets and masks, as well as jewellery and ceramics. *Jl Raya Ubud.* ☎ *(0361) 971 997. MC, V. Map p. 141.*

Beachwear

★★★ Blue Glue SEMINYAK

Bikinis like you've never seen them before. There are some practical ones, but others have so many flounces, flowers and even sequined angel wings that I'm sure they're never meant to get wet. *Jl Raya Bansangkasa 6.* ☎ *(0361) 844 5956. MC, V. Map p. 140.*

Drifter SEMINYAK   Everything for the well-dressed surfer, including surf boards, board shorts, T-shirts galore, and even surfing books and old surfing magazine posters. *Jl Laksmana 50 (Jl Oberoi).* ☎ *(0361) 733 274. MC, V. Map p. 140.*

Surfer Girl KUTA   Teenage girls can't get enough of this store crammed with pretty bikinis and other beachwear. Five stores are located in Kuta and Legian, and one in Nusa Dua. *Kuta Square.* ☎ *(0361) 753 885. MC, V. Map p. 139.*

The finished products.

Surfer girl, a chain of shops crammed with pretty bikinis and other beachwear.

Clothing & Accessories

★★ Dari Bali UBUD   The only thing sold here are handbags, but what sublime bags they are—elegant handwoven baskets from Tenganan in Eastern Bali. *Jl Hanoman 23.* ☎ *081 999 315 285. No credit cards. Map p. 141.*

Harmonis UBUD   Stylish linen clothing that you can wear once you get home and it won't scream 'I've been to Bali too!' *Monkey Forest Rd (Jl Wenara Wana).* ☎ *(0361) 972 691. No credit cards. Map p. 141.*

Lulu Yasmine SEMINYAK   Need to pick up something glamorous to fit in with the fashionistas at Ku De Ta? Lulu Yasmine has exactly what you need. Lots of sexy little dresses perfect for Seminyak's party scene. There's another location at Jl Raya Seminyak 53 (☎ (0361) 732 711). *Jl Laksmana 100X (Jl Oberoi).* ☎ *(0361) 736-763. AE, MC, V. Map p. 140.*

Milo's Bazaar SEMINYAK   Local designer Milo Migliavacca is one of Bali's best, and his party dresses in brightly painted silk and other floaty fabrics are hard to resist. *Jl Laksmana 38 (Jl Oberoi).* ☎ *(0361) 735 551. AE, MC, V. Map p. 140.*

Morena SEMINYAK Chic beach-wear and party clothes with lots of floaty flounces. *Jl Laksmana 69 (Jl Oberoi).* ☎ *(0361) 745 3531. MC, V. Map p. 140.*

★★★ Paul Ropp SEMINYAK
Paul Ropp is one of Bali's most well-known high-end fashion designers. His clothes are bold, bright and very colourful and channel the 60s hippy chic movement. The range extends from frilly knickers to bags and shoes (beaded velvet boots any-one?), beachwear, evening wear and smart casual. I love the patch-work trilbys. *Jl Laksmana (Jl Oberoi).* ☎ *(0361) 734 208. AE, MC, V. Map p. 140.*

Paul's Place SEMINYAK If you're tired of falling in love with a piece of clothing only to find out the larg-est size on the rack is a 6, head to Paul's. The softly draped dresses and tops are designed with the fuller figure in mind. The only draw-back is that most of the range is in either black or white. *Jl Laksmana 18B (Jl Oberoi).* ☎ *(0361) 736 910. MC, V. Map p. 140.*

Rai Sandi UBUD The designs are traditional Bali, with lots of batik and batik-inspired prints, but the fabrics are good quality. It's the perfect place to pick up a gossamer-thin silk

Paul Ropp, one of Bali's most well-known high-end fashion designers.

scarf or a soft silky robe. It also has good range of cotton sarongs that are much better than the ones you'll find in markets and street stalls. *Jl Raya Sanggingan.* ☎ *(0361) 975 119. AE, MC, V. Map p. 141.*

Sei-Sui UBUD On the off chance that you've come to Bali in search of a vintage Japanese kimono, this is the place to go. The silk gowns are absolutely beautiful. *Jl Raya Sang-gingan* ☎ *(0361) 794 5153. V. Map p. 141.*

Shibana SEMINYAK Blinged-up beaded and sequined thongs and sandals at bargain prices. Most of the shoes are in bags rather than on display, so you'll need to spend some time sorting through them, but the hunt is worth it. *Jl Raya Basangkasa 42.* ☎ *(0361) 736 770. No credit cards. Map p. 140.*

sks SEMINYAK sks stands for sim-ple konsep sale and the range of men's and women's smart casual wear will get you anywhere. But the real reason I love this store is for the adorable little dolls made out of string (50 000Rp). All proceeds go to help the street kids of Bali (for details, see www.ykpa.org). *Jl Laks-mana 40 (Jl Oberoi).* ☎ *(0361) 361 1124. AE, MC, V. Map p. 140.*

Books
Ganesha Bookshop UBUD
The front of the store sells second-hand books, mostly of the thriller/romance and easy holiday reading type, but the back section has a fantastic collection of books on and about Bali, ranging from guidebooks to fiction, history, architecture and academia. *Jl Raya Ubud.* ☎ *(0361) 973 359. AE, MC, V. Map p. 141.*

★★ Periplus TUBAN, UBUD This great English-language bookshop chain has a decent selection of books that goes beyond the airport

Adorable little dolls for sale at sks. All proceeds from the sales of the dolls go to help the street kids of Bali.

thriller range you'll find in most bookshops in Kuta. It's the place to go if you're looking for quality books about Bali. It also has a section for kids, and sells international newspapers and magazines as well. Two stores are located in the Kuta area, one in Discovery Mall, the other in Bali Galleria (Jl Ngurah Rai Bypass, ☎ (0361) 752-670), and there's also branches in Seminyak and Ubud, as well as at the airport. *Ubud: Monkey Forest Rd (Jl Wenara Wana. ☎ (0361) 975 178. Map p. 149; Tuban: Discovery Mall, Jl Kartika Plaza. ☎ (0361) 769 757. AE, MC, V. Map p. 139.*

Department Stores & Malls

Bali Galleria KUTA   All the big name international brands (Dior, Bulgari, Fendi, Gucci, Burberry and so on) in one huge mall and a large duty-free shop. It's popular, particularly with tour groups, but I'm not really sure why—as far as I'm concerned it's the same stuff you can get anywhere around the world at much the same prices. *Jl Ngurah Rai Bypass. Map p. 139.*

Discovery Mall TUBAN   It's full of all the high street brands you'll find at home in your local mall, at very similar prices, but it is right on the water's edge (quite literally) and there's several large stores selling quality Balinese design and souvenirs. It's a good option if you want to escape into some air-conditioned comfort for a while and browse without the constant attention and need to haggle that you get in the smaller shops on the street. *Jl Kartika Plaza. www.discoveryshopping mall.com. Map p. 139.*

Matahari KUTA   Forgotten something? Desperately need a new suitcase to take home all your bargains? This department store and supermarket has everything you need, from groceries, homewares and cooking utensils to luggage, cosmetics, shoes and just about everything else. The ground floor is dedicated to souvenirs. *Kuta Sq. Map p. 139.*

Fabric

Lucy's Batik SEMINYAK   A treasure trove of batik of all kinds, some traditional, some creatively modern, in both cotton and silk. There's a range of clothes and pillows, but most of the fabric is in lengths large enough to make your own things when you get home. *Jl Raya Basangkasa 88. ☎ (0361) 795 1275. MC, V. Map p. 140.*

★★★ Pasar Badung DENPASAR The third level of this huge market in downtown Denpasar is the place to buy fabric of any description, although it's geared to local tastes rather than tourists. Spend enough time looking and you'll be sure to find something to your taste. If you can't, try neighbouring Jl Sulawesi, which is lined with fabric shops. *Jl Gajah Mada. Map p. 142.*

★★★ Threads of Life UBUD More like a museum than a shop, this Indonesian Textile Arts Centre displays exquisite museum-quality

Threads of Life, displaying exquisite museum-quality batik and weaving.

batik and weaving from all over Indonesia, and everything you see on the walls is also for sale. There's a small educational display at the front, which shows you how the clothes are made, and if you want to know more, you can join a class on Tuesday or Wednesday morning (two-hour classes cost 150000Rp). *Jl Kajeng 24.* ☎ *(0361) 972 187. www.threadsoflife.com. AE, MC, V. Map p. 141.*

Homewares

Ashitaba SEMINYAK Beautiful handwoven baskets from the Aga village in Tenganan in Eastern Bali. There are some purses, but also lots of containers and bowls. *Jl Raya Seminyak 6.* ☎ *(0361) 737 054. MC, V. Map p. 140.*

Haveli SEMINYAK If your house (or your neck and wrists) needs some bling, this is the place to find it. Beaded cushions, white feather lampshades and more bits and baubles for your table than you can count. *Jl Raya Basangkasa 38.* ☎ *(0361) 737 160. AE, MC, V. Map p. 140.*

Tanda Mata UBUD Tanda Mata sells a range of quality homewares, with everything from elegant leather desk sets for your office, to wooden frames and trays, brass door knockers, ceramics and glassware, plus a small selection of jewellery. *Jl Raya Ubud.* ☎ *(0361) 978 547. AE, MC, V. Map p. 141.*

Toko East UBUD Candles, vases and ceramics are the best items in this little store. It also has a small range of Balinese chill out music to help you re-create the Bali vibe at home. *Jl Raya Ubud.* ☎ *(0361) 978 306. AE, MC, V. Map p. 141.*

★★ Wibisana SEMINYAK If you want to create your own Balinese garden when you get home, you're going to need a couple of silk umbrellas and this little store is the place to get them. They'll even cut them in half (and tell you how to put them back together) and box them up, so you can check them in as oversized luggage for the trip home. *Jl Raya Basangkasa 7.* ☎ *(0361) 874 9974. No credit cards. Map p. 140.*

Jewellery

Maha Blanco Jewellery UBUD Most art museum gift shops sell art books or reproductions, but the shop at Blanco Renaissance Museum just sells gorgeous jewellery designed by the artist's youngest daughter, Maha Blanco. The range is all silver, and many pieces feature pearls or turquoise. *Jl Raya Campuan.* ☎ *(0361) 975 502. AE, MC, V. Map p. 141.*

Sea Gypsy SEMINYAK Lots of silver and pearls, including the famous Lombok black pearls. There's another store at Jl Raya Seminyak 30X (☎ (0361) 847 5765). *Jl Laksmana 49 (Jl Oberoi).* ☎ *(0361) 731 769. MC, V. Map p. 140.*

Silver CELUK   Ninety per cent of the people who live in Celuk make silver and gold jewellery for a living—it's the silver centre of Bali and there are literally hundreds of showrooms on the main road and surrounding backstreets. Most tours to Ubud or the volcano stop at a showroom en route. Fixed prices are high, but they usually start with a hefty discount and you can bargain harder after that. If you want something made to order, it's best to visit on your own and try one of the smaller workshops for lower prices. *Map p. 142.*

Studio Perak UBUD   Original silver jewellery made by local artists, including inmates of the infamous Kerobokan Jail as part of a rehabilitation program. The designs are fresh and not super expensive. If you'd like to make your own, it runs three-hour jewellery-making classes for 250 000Rp. *Jl Raya Ubud.* ☎ *(0361) 973 371. AE, MC, V. Map p. 141.*

Markets
Pasar Sari Meta Nadi LEGIAN It's rather euphemistically called an art market, but the 'art' extends to cheap woodcarvings (a multitude of wooden penis bottle openers among them), churned out canvases that are the same in every stall,

Some of the wares at Studio Perak, where they sell original silver jewellery made by local artists, including inmates of the infamous Kerobokan Jail as part of a rehabilitation program.

trinkets and other souvenirs. There are hundreds of Bintang and 'I ♥ Bali' T-shirts and bags and cheap sarongs. Bargain hard if you do find something you like. *Jl Melasti. Map p. 139.*

★★ Pasar Ubud UBUD   You'll find hundreds of tiny stalls selling souvenirs, clothing, costume jewellery, bags and 'art' in this market place spread over two levels in the heart of Ubud. It's mostly tourist tat, but you can pick it up dirt cheap as long as you bargain hard. It can get hot and crowded inside, and the aisles are barely wide enough for one person to squeeze through, let alone two going in opposite directions, but it's a lot of fun. *Jl Raya Ubud, opposite the Ubud Palace. Map p. 141.*

Haveli, the place to find glamorous housewares.

Music & Instruments

Moari UBUD   Drums, gongs, bells, wooden flutes and rattles—you'll find all manner of musical instrument here, as well as a good selection of CDs of both traditional and contemporary Balinese and Indonesian music, including some nice chill-out compilations. *Jl Raya Ubud.* ☎ *(0361) 977 367. No credit cards. Map p. 141.*

Pondok Bamboo Music Shop UBUD   From the outside it looks as if all this little shop opposite the Monkey Forest sells is bamboo wind chimes, but head down the back and you'll find some gorgeous gamelan instruments. The owner, Nyoman Warsa, is a well-known gamelan musician. He also stages shadow puppet shows here on Mondays and Thursdays at 8pm (75 000Rp). *Monkey Forest Rd (Jl Wenara Wana).* ☎ *(0361) 974 807. MC, V. Map p. 141.*

Souvenirs

★ **Flying Dragon** UBUD   Handmade and hand-painted Balinese kites of every type and description. These kites, some of which are a work of art, make a great souvenir, and can look just as good on a wall as high in the sky. *Jl Raya Ubud.* ☎ *(0361) 805 6850. No credit cards. Map p. 141.*

Painted wooden eggs on sale.

Beautiful kites make a great souvenir.

★★★ **Pasar Kumbasari** DENPASAR   Three levels of art, craft and souvenir bliss. It's a wholesale as well as a retail art and handicraft market, so this is where most of the stuff you see in your resort or hotel shop, as well as most of the stores in Kuta, Legian and Nusa Dua, is sourced from. This means you can often get a better price, but you'll need to bargain hard. *Jl Gajah Mada. Map p. 142.*

Tegun Folk Art Gallery UBUD   This crowded showroom is a cut above your average souvenir shop. You'll find a huge range of high quality arts and craft from all over Bali and Indonesia. Most of it is handmade, so it's not the same old stuff you see everywhere else. *Jl Hanoman 44.* ☎ *(0361) 970 581. MC, V. Map p. 141.*

Yoga Gear

The Yoga Shop UBUD   Arrived in Ubud without your yoga gear? Don't panic. This little shop stocks everything you need. *Jl Hanoman (near Tegun Gallery).* ☎ *(0361) 970 992. MC, V. Map p. 141.* ●

Nightlife **Best Bets**

An aerial view of the Rock Bar.

Best **All Night Party**
Bounty *Jl Legian, Legian (p. 158)*

Best **Celebrity Spotting**
★★★ Ku De Ta *Jl Laksmana (Jl Oberoi), Seminyak (p. 157)*

Best **Cocktails**
★ Hu'u *Jl Pantai Kaya Aya, Seminyak (p. 156)*

Best **Jazz**
Jazz Cafe *Jl Sukma 2, Ubud (p. 159)*

Most **Laid-back**
Warung Rasta *Jl Kubu Gembong, Lovina (p. 160)*

Best **Rock**
Hard Rock Cafe *Jl Pantai Kuta, Kuta (p. 159)*

Best **Spooky Dance Venue**
★★ Pura Dalem *Jl Raya Ubud, Ubud (p. 156)*

Best **View**
★★★ The Rock Bar *Jl Karang Mas Sejahtera, Jimbaran (p. 158)*

Best **Wine Bar**
★★★ Sip Wine Bar *Jl Raya Seminyak 16A, Seminyak (p. 157)*

Previous page: Sunset at Ku De Ta.

Kuta & Legian Nightlife

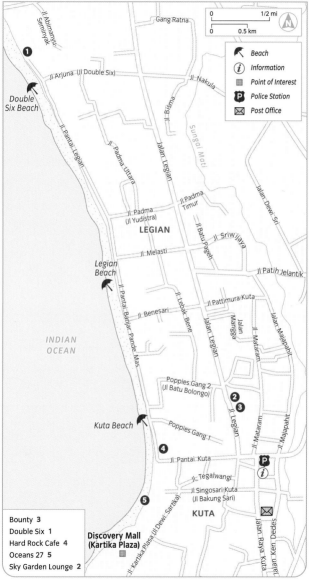

Gang Ratna

Jl Abimanyu-Seminyak

Jl Arjuna (Jl Double Six)

Jl Nakula

Double Six Beach

Jl Pantai Legian

Jl Bisma

Jalan Legian

Jl Padma Uttara

Jl Padma Timur

Jl Padma (Jl Yudistra)

LEGIAN

Jl Batu Pageh

Jl Sriwijaya

Jl Melasti

Jl Patih Jelantik

Legian Beach

Jalan Dewi Sri

Jl Pantai Banjar Pande Mas

Jl Benesari

Jl Lebak-Bene

Jl Pattimura-Kuta

Jalan Mangga

Jalan Legian

Jalan Mataram

Jalan Majapahit

INDIAN OCEAN

Poppies Gang 2 (Jl Batu Bolongo)

❷
❸

Jl Legian

Kuta Beach

Poppies Gang 1

❹

Jl Pantai Kuta

Jl Tegalwangi

Jl Singosari-Kuta (Jl Bakung Sari)

KUTA

Jalan Ken Dedes

Jalan Raya Kuta

❺

Jl Kartika Plaza (Jl Dewi Sartika)

Discovery Mall (Kartika Plaza)

0   1/2 mi
0   0.5 km

- 🏖 Beach
- ⓘ Information
- ▪ Point of Interest
- 🅿 Police Station
- ✉ Post Office

Bounty **3**
Double Six **1**
Hard Rock Cafe **4**
Oceans 27 **5**
Sky Garden Lounge **2**

Seminyak Nightlife

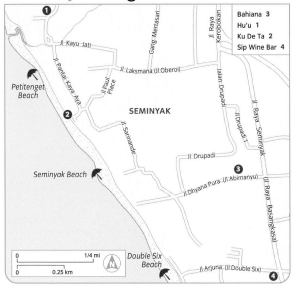

Bahiana 3
Hu'u 1
Ku De Ta 2
Sip Wine Bar 4

Ubud Nightlife

Café Lotus 2
Jazz Cafe 5
Pura Batu Karu 3
Pura Dalem Ubud 1
Ubud Palace 4

Around the Island Nightlife

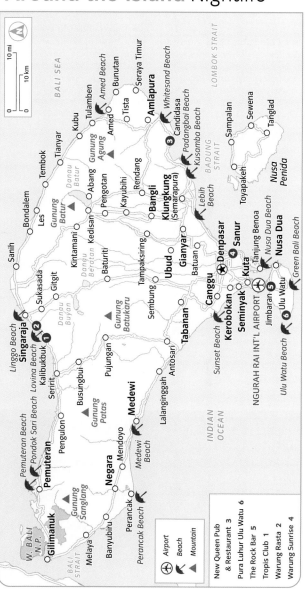

New Queen Pub & Restaurant **3**
Pura Luhur Ulu Watu **6**
The Rock Bar **5**
Tropis Club **1**
Warung Rasta **2**
Warung Sunrise **4**

Bali Nightlife A to Z

Balinese Dance & Music

★★ Café Lotus UBUD Traditional Balinese performances are staged every evening, except Wednesdays and Fridays, and cost 80 000Rp, but for this you get a front row table at one of the most beautiful venues in Ubud, overlooking a sublime lotus lily pond in front of Pura Taman Saraswati. *Jl Raya Ubud.* 🕿 *(0361) 975 660. Map p. 154.*

★ Pura Batu Karu UBUD They're not as polished as some performances, but there's a Kecak Fire and Trance Dance every Sunday and Thursday, and all money goes towards the building of a new temple. Shows start at 7.30pm and cost 75 000Rp. *Jl Suweta. Map p. 154.*

★★ Pura Dalem Ubud UBUD The Temple of the Dead can be a spooky place to watch a Kecak Fire and Trance Dance, but there's something on here every night of the week, including Legong and gamelan orchestras. Shows start at either 7pm or 7.30pm and cost 65 000Rp to 75 000Rp. *Jl Raya Ubud. Map p. 154.*

★★ Pura Luhur Ulu Watu ULU WATU The Kecak Fire and Trance Dance is a bit more touristy here than those staged at Ubud, but the setting is magic, even though it's performed during the daylight hours rather than in darkness. Shows start at 6pm and cost 70 000Rp. *Map p. 155.*

★★★ Ubud Palace UBUD One of the most atmospheric places to see a traditional dance performance in Ubud. There's a performance of either Legong or Barong every night. Shows start at 7.30pm and cost 80 000Rp. *Corner of Jl Raya Ubud and Jl Suweta. Map p. 154.*

Bars & Lounges

★ Hu'u SEMINYAK Like Ku De Ta (see opposite), Hu'u is a hybrid of restaurant, lounge and nightclub. Without a beach. Head here before midnight for devilishly delicious lychee martinis, but have one too many and you'll find yourself still here in the pre-dawn hours burning up the dance floor. *Jl Pantai Kaya Aya.* 🕿 *(0361) 736 443. Map p. 154.*

If you see only one dance in Bali, make it a Kecak dance.

Which dance?

There are dozens of different traditional dances in Bali; some are slow and sensuous, others dramatic and full of energy. The three most popular you are likely to see are the Legong, Barong and Kecak. Performances, unless noted otherwise, are always outdoors, subject to weather, and you'll be seated on plastic chairs. Arrive early to secure the best position.

The **Legong** dance is traditionally performed by young girls elaborately made up and dressed in beautiful costumes, often gold brocade. It's highly stylised and very graceful, with intricate hand movements, but some young children may lose interest after the first half-hour or so.

The **Barong** dance features the shaggy beast that is half dog, half lion, and it's always a hit with children, not just for the colourful costumes but for the action and drama that anyone can follow. Most dances involve the Barong doing battle with the equally hairy but evil fang-toothed witch Rangda, who always gets it in the end.

If you only see one dance in Bali, make it a **Kecak** dance. There's no music; a choir of men sit in a circle and chant themselves into a trance-like state, while various scenes from the Hindu epic, the Ramayana, are acted out. See this performed in a darkened temple and the atmosphere is electrifying, the chanting quite mesmerising. Most performances culminate in a fire dance, when the dancer, in a trance, dances on a bed of hot coals. Yes, the fire is real, and no, I don't know how he does it without burning the soles of his feet off.

★★★ **Ku De Ta** SEMINYAK
Home to most of Bali's best parties, this beachside bar is where the bold and beautiful go to rub shoulders with other bold and beautiful. It's open all day, with daybeds and chill-out music perfect for a sun-soaked lunch, but it's for sunset cocktails and starlight dancing that it's most renowned for. Dress up in your best party gear and don't forget your credit card. *Jl Laksmana (Jl Oberoi).* ☎ *(0361) 736 969. Map p. 154.*

★★★ **Oceans 27** TUBAN   If you want to watch the sun slip into the sea with a cocktail in your hand, this stylish bar with prime beachfront views is the place to go. You're spoilt for choice on where to sit:

either at a table, a lounge on the sundeck, lying back on the cushions in your own cabana on the sand, or maybe cooling your heels at a half-submerged table and chair in the pool. If you get peckish, there's a tapas menu, or go for pizza or a grill. *Beachfront, Discovery Shopping Mall, Jl Kartika Plaza.* ☎ *(0361) 767 300. Map p. 153.*

★★★ **Sip Wine Bar** SEMINYAK
With a horrendous tax imposed on imported wine, good wine bars, or even good wine lists for that matter, are pretty much nonexistent in Bali. Except for Sip, that is. It's chic and stylish and expensive, but if you like your wine, and you prefer to eat, drink and talk the night away, as

A mask from the Barong dance, a hit with the children.

opposed to twist and shout, then I can guarantee you'll be back more than once. The food, Classic French Bistro fare, is also excellent. *Jl Raya Seminyak 16A.* ☎ *(0361) 730 810. Map p. 154.*

★★★ The Rock Bar JIMBARAN I normally wouldn't suggest going out of your way just to visit a hotel bar, particularly when it's not really within walking distance (or even an easy taxi ride) of anything else, but the Rock Bar at Ayana Resort is

Oceans 27, a prime spot to watch the sunset with a cocktail in your hand.

different. Hanging out over the water halfway up a cliff, this bar has views you have to see to believe. Dress up, try and look like you belong and go here for sunset at least once. *Jl Karang Mas Sejahtera.* ☎ *(0361) 702 222. www.ayana resort.com. Map p. 155.*

Live Music & Dance Clubs

Bahiana SEMINYAK You could be forgiven for thinking that someone has spiked your drink and you've woken up in the Caribbean, because this place is all about rum drinks and salsa. Some of the parties are a little bit daggy, but it's a good place to perfect your dance steps—the free salsa lessons help. *Jl Dhyana Pura (Jl Abimanyu).* ☎ *(0361) 738 662. Map p. 154.*

Bounty KUTA Shiver me timbers me hearties, thar'll be plenty of scallywags loaded to the gunwales by morning light in this fine ship. Act out your worst pirate fantasies aboard the Bounty, which heaves with disco, techno and pop all night long, from midnight until dawn. *Jl Legian.* ☎ *(0361) 752 529. Map p. 153.*

Double Six KUTA One of the longest-running nightclubs in Bali, no one's quite sure anymore whether the club was named after the beach,

The Rock Bar hangs over the water halfway up a cliff; it has views you have to see to believe.

or if it was the other way round. Go for sunset drinks and stay until the sun-up dancing in the open-air pavilion. *Jl Arjuna (Jl Double Six).* ☎ *(0361) 733 067. Map p. 153.*

Hard Rock Cafe KUTA   Live rock and roll almost every night of the week, this is the place to see visiting rocks stars (and a few wannabes). Make sure you're ready to dance because the air conditioning can be icy sometimes. *Jl Pantai Kuta.* ☎ *(0361) 761 869. Map p. 153.*

Jazz Cafe UBUD   Grab a cocktail or a glass of wine and kickback with live jazz nightly (except Mondays) from 7.30pm to 10.30pm in a lovely palm-filled garden setting. Tuesdays are smooth and mellow, Wednesdays have a Latin Groove, Thursdays are all about fusion and funk, as are Fridays, with a little acid jazz thrown in, Saturdays are R&B and Sundays are acoustic. *Jl Sukma 2.* ☎ *(0361) 976 594. Cover 25000Rp (free if you spend more than 150000Rp per person on food and drink). Map p. 154.*

Bounty, where disco, techno and pop blare all night long.

Warung Sunrise, your destination for live reggae.

New Queen Pub & Restaurant

CANDIDASA   There's not a lot of choice when it comes to nightlife in Candidasa that doesn't involve a Legong dance, except for the very laid-back New Queen, which livens up on Wednesday and Saturday nights with live acoustic music from 7pm to 9pm. Expect more than your fair share of reggae, but the band is happy to take requests if you want something else. *Jl Raya Candidasa.* ☎ *0812 3653 1832. Map p. 155.*

Sky Garden Lounge KUTA

There are three floors of lounges and dance floors at Sky Garden, but the best is the rooftop bar, where you'll find some of the best DJs in town. *Jl Legian 61.* ☎ *(0361) 756 362. Map p. 164.*

Tropis Club LOVINA   One of the

few places on Lovina beach that offers live music—even it's just one of the locals playing a guitar and singing some old 80s favourites. But for Lovina, this is about as racy as night-time entertainment gets.

Jl Ketapang. ☎ *(0362) 42090. Map p. 155.*

Warung Rasta LOVINA   Nightlife

in Anturan is pretty much MYOF (Make Your Own Fun). If you're lucky, the local lads will be building a bonfire on the beach and singing some songs and more than happy to have you join in. But if all else fails, Warung Rasta serves up a steady diet of reggae along with some fabulous dirt-cheap seafood. *On the beach at the end of Jl Kubu Gembong.* ☎ *No phone. Map p. 155.*

Warung Sunrise SANUR   This

little beachside bar and restaurant on the sandy beach at Sanur might be named for the dawn, but it's most popular once the sun goes down, with live reggae from 8.30pm on Mondays, Wednesdays and Fridays. Every other night of the week it's nonstop Bob Marley on the sound system. *Beach Promenade (Jl Hang Tuah Pantai).* ☎ *0813 3809 0486. Map p. 155.* ●

The **Savvy**
Traveller

Before You Go

Government Tourist Offices

You'll find plenty of places in tourist areas across Bali with signs announcing that they offer tourist information. They are tour sellers. The only real tourist information centre is in Ubud, but even then, staff seem to spend more time booking tours than providing free information, although they do offer some excellent cultural and walking tours. The office is opposite Ubud Palace on the corner of Jl Raya Ubud and Monkey Forest Rd; officially Jl Wenara Wana ((0361) 973 285). There is also a government website: www.balitourismboard.org. Another good source of information is the *Bali Advertiser,* a free fortnightly newspaper that caters mainly to the expat crowd but can be useful. You pick up it up at bars and shops throughout Southern Bali.

The Best Time to Go

Bali is just 8 degrees below the equator, which means it's always hot and mostly steamy. High season is around Christmas and July (especially during Australian school holidays) and August, when it can get very busy and accommodation can be booked solid. April and September have the best combination of good weather and light crowds, but be aware if you are in Bali on Nyepi (see Festivals & Special Events below), the whole island shuts down and you will be confined to your hotel for the day.

Festivals & Special Events

There seems to be almost always a temple ceremony or village festival happening in Bali, so chances are you'll encounter one at some stage during your trip. Two of the biggest

are the 10-day **Galungan Ceremony** (July 2011, February 2012, August 2013), when gods and ancestors visit the earth, good triumphs over evil and *barongs* (big shaggy lion monsters) dance from village to village amid general festivities and feasting. Ten days later is the **Kuningan Ceremony**, when the gods go back to heaven and temples, homes and streets everywhere are decorated with bamboo ornaments.

Other major festivals include the following:

MAR–APR. We might celebrate the new year with lots of loud partying, but the **Balinese New Year** is observed in silence.

Nyepi (the Day of Silence) falls on the day following the dark moon of the spring equinox and marks the beginning of the Hindu new year, usually sometime between mid-March and early April (March 5, 2011, March 23, 2012, March 12, 2013). For 24 hours, starting at sunrise, the whole island shuts down. The airport is closed, no vehicles can be operated, no TVs can be watched, no lights turned on. All businesses (except hotels and hospitals) are closed and no one is allowed to walk the streets. The idea is that the silence will fool any bad spirits into believing the island is empty and they will go elsewhere. The rules apply to tourists as well as locals, although the rules are a little more relaxed as long as you stay inside your hotel, which will provide room service for the day.

Three days before Nyepi all the effigies of the gods from all the village temples are taken to the nearest river, lake or ocean for a ritual cleansing. On the day before Nyepi, all villages in Bali hold a large exorcism ceremony

BALI'S AVERAGE TEMPERATURE & RAINFALL

	JAN	FEB	MAR	APR	MAY	JUN
Daily temp (°C)	32	32	32	33	33	31
Daily temp (°F)	90	90	90	91	91	88
Avg Rainfall (mm)	300	280	215	100	85	75

	JUL	AUG	SEP	OCT	NOV	DEC
Daily temp (°C)	31	31	32	33	32	32
Daily temp (°F)	88	88	90	91	90	90
Avg Rainfall (mm)	55	40	90	100	150	295

at the main village cross road, believed to be the meeting place of demons. Fantastic monsters, called *Ogoh-ogoh,* made of bamboo and sporting terrifying fangs, bulging eyes and wild hair, are brought to the crossroads with flaming torches amid a noisy cacophony of drum banging, yelling, screaming and fireworks to scare the evil spirits away. Any demons left will be so bored by the silence the next day they leave of their own accord.

JUN–JUL. The month-long **Bali Arts Festival** usually kicks off in mid-June in Denpasar at the Arts Centre and is a great opportunity to see Bali's best traditional dancers and musicians perform (www.baliartsfestival. com).

The skies over Sanur fill with kites of all descriptions in July (sometimes August) for the annual **Bali Kite Festival**, when giant fish-, bird- and leaf-shaped kites, some more than 10m in length, are flown by teams of up to 10 or more kite fliers to encourage the Gods to provide a good harvest.

SEPT–OCT. Kuta parties even more than normal with a 10-day celebration of traditional dances in the streets and various activities designed to entertain tourists during the **Kuta Karnival** (www.kuta karnival.com).

Bookworms should high tail it to Ubud for the annual **Ubud Writers & Readers Festival,** a four-day festival of book readings, author talks, workshops, readings and more that attracts high-profile writers, and readers, from around the world (www.ubudwritersfestival.com).

The Weather

You can swim year-round in Bali, and you'll never need a jacket, unless you're heading into the mountain-top villages of Kintamani or Candikuning, where it does get cold. The wet season is officially October to March, but it can, and does, rain at any time of the year, although not usually for long. If you're heading to Bali for the surf, it's also good year-round, although best conditions are typically between May and August. Ubud is cooler than the southern beach areas, and is pleasantly chilled at night-time, at least cool enough to forgo air conditioning at any rate.

Useful Websites

- **www.balidiscovery.com:** Hotels, deals, tours and useful tips.

- **www.baliadvertiser.biz:** Online version of the free expat newspaper.

- **www.balieats.com:** Restaurant reviews.

- **www.asiarooms.com:** Book accommodation at more than 480 hotels and resorts.

- **www.balivillas.com:** Private villa rentals.

Cell Phones (Mobiles)

Bali, like Australia, is on the GSM network, so as long as your mobile phone (called a handphone in Bali), is world capable and you have activated global roaming (contact your service provider to check), you should be able to make and receive calls pretty much anywhere in Bali. Not all North American phones are GSM, but you can rent one before leaving home from **InTouch U.S.A.** (☎ (800) 872 7626; www.intouchglobal.com) or **RoadPost** (☎ (888) 290 1606/ (905) 272 5665; www.roadpost.com). InTouch will also, for free, advise you on whether your existing phone will work overseas; call ☎ (703) 222 7161 between 9am and 4pm EST, or go to http://intouchglobal.com/travel.htm. If you plan on making a lot of calls, consider buying a local prepaid SIM card in Bali for more attractive call costs, but make sure you phone is unlocked (ie: not locked to a particular provider or telco) before you leave home. SIM cards are sold everywhere.

Visas

The rules concerning visas seem to change on a regular basis, so always check the current situation before you leave home. There a handful of countries that don't require a visa (including Chile, Brunei Darussalam, Hong Kong, Macau, Malaysia, Morocco, Peru, Philippines, Singapore, Thailand and Vietnam) but most countries, including Australia, New Zealand, the UK and USA, can obtain a visa on arrival as long as

your passport has more than six-months validity and at least two blank pages and you have proof of a return, or forward, plane ticket. It will cost US$25 and is only payable in US currency, so make sure you have some US notes when you arrive to save mucking about. These visas are good for 30 days and cannot be extended. If you want to stay longer, you will need to obtain a visa from your nearest Indonesian embassy or consulate before you arrive. You can find a list at www.deplu.go.id (go to the mission section).

Books on Bali

There are hundreds of books out there either on or about Bali. *Eat Pray Love*, by Elizabeth Gilbert, is the hugely popular account of an American woman's attempt to find inner peace in Italy, India and finally Bali, Ubud in particular. Julia Roberts starred in the recent movie. It's loved and hated by readers in equal measure (I found it tedious and difficult to finish) but make up your own mind. A much more captivating read is Colin McPhee's *A House In Bali*, also set in Ubud. Composer McPhee lived in Ubud in the 1930s and was fascinated by gamelan music and his charming book provides delightful insights into the culture, music and traditions of Bali before the onslaught of tourism. It can be hard to find, but *Our Hotel in Bali* by Louise Koke is also set in the 1930s. Koke and her photographer husband, Bob, built and ran the first hotel in Kuta. The photographs of a vanished Bali are amazing (if you can't find the book, which is long out of print, there are prints of some of the photos on display at the Neka Art Museum in Ubud; see p. 31, bullet ❶). For an examination of some of the issues facing contemporary Bali, Emma Tom's *Bali: Paradise Lost?* offers a unique perspective from a distinctively Australian point of view.

Getting **There**

By Plane
Ngurah Rai Airport, most commonly called Denpasar airport, is only a few kilometres south of Kuta—you can see the runway from some sections of the beach at Jimbaran. There are two terminals, international and domestic, a few hundred metres apart. Currency exchange offices and ATMs are available at both.

Although arrival procedures are straightforward, it can take an inexplicably long time to get to the head of the immigration queue—waits of up to two hours are not unusual, so be prepared with comfortable shoes, a bottle of water, a good book, toys for the kids and a large supply of patience. It's very crowded and the hall is not air conditioned, so it can get very hot. If you've come from somewhere cold, make sure you can peel off some layers. The ever-entrepreneurial Balinese have come up with a service that will fast track the formalities and whisk away your passports to be stamped on your behalf while you wait in an air-conditioned lounge for the princely sum of US$35 per person. I've always been too stingy to pay, and always wished I had when sweating it out in the excruciatingly long and inexorably slow-moving line. Ask your travel agent or hotel if they offer the service when booking, or organise it yourself via www.balivipservice.com.

Be wary of helpful porters once you finally make it through customs—if you don't want to pay for their services, don't let them carry your bag, even if they insist.

Many hotels offer free transport to and from the airport, especially if you're staying for two or more nights, so always ask when booking. However, if they offer the service for a charge (often US$10 or US$15), it's worth comparing the price to the fixed-price taxi ticket you can buy from the official Ngurah Rai taxi counter outside the international terminal, which displays its prices on the wall. A fare to Kuta will cost 50 000Rp, Sanur or Nusa Dua 95 000Rp and Ubud 195 000Rp. Surfboards will cost around 35 000Rp extra. Beware of drivers offering rides in taxis other than Ngurah Rai—they are operating illegally and it will be harder to negotiate a reasonable fare. Getting to the airport, where you can use any taxi you choose, is usually much cheaper.

Airlines that fly direct to Bali from Australia include the Indonesian national carrier, Garuda, Air Asia, Jetstar and Pacific Blue. You can also fly direct to Bali from Bangkok with Thai Airways, Singapore with Singapore Airlines and Lion Air, Tokyo with Japan Airlines, Malaysia with Malaysia Airlines and Air Asia, and Hong Kong with Cathay Pacific. See 'Phone Numbers & Websites' on p. 177 for contact information.

By Ferry
If travelling to Bali by ferry from Lombok, you'll arrive at either Benoa or Padangbai and will usually be met by shuttle buses and taxis. If you're coming from Java, you'll arrive at Gilimanuk in Western Bali where you can pick up a local bus to Denpasar or Singaraja on the north coast. Don't expect air conditioning.

Getting **Around**

Finding an address in Bali can be a challenge. Many small streets and laneways (called *gangs*) don't have a name, and even when they do they may not be signposted. Not that signposting always helps—many Balinese streets are known by two names. Traditionally, they are named after a well-known business, landmark or temple that is either on (or near) the street, but officially they will have different name. Confusingly either name can be used in the address. Examples include Jl Oberoi in Seminyak, which is also Jl Laksmana, Jl Double Six (Jl Arjuna) and Monkey Forest Rd in Ubud, which is officially Jl Wenara Wana. We have included both street names where applicable in the addresses in this guide.

By Bus

Getting around Bali by public transport is cheap, but slow and circuitous. While there are some larger buses that travel the 'long distance' (by Balinese standards) route from Denpasar to the ferry terminal in Gilimanuk, on the far west coast, and Bali's second-largest city, Singaraja, on the north coast, most locals that don't have their own transport travel by **bemo** (minibus). There's no set schedule or even route, you just flag one down, negotiate a price (usually a few thousand rupiah), squeeze yourself in and hope that there aren't too many stops or detours along the way—which all depends on where your fellow passengers want to go. In Southern Bali you'll have to hub in and out of Denpasar, as there are no direct services between tourist towns such as Kuta and Sanur, for example.

A slightly more comfortable and quicker alternative if you are travelling from one tourist area to another is a **tourist shuttle**, which you'll find advertised everywhere. They'll usually pick you up from your hotel and drop you in a central location at your destination, but you may have to wait until they have a minimum number of passengers. You should always take advertised departure times as a guide, rather than gospel.

A slightly cheaper option (although much more expensive than a bemo) is a **Perama tourist shuttle bus**. Pick up and drop off is at its offices (Kuta, Sanur, Ubud, Lovina, Padangbai and Candidasa) and they are usually on time, although the journeys are not always direct. A trip from Candidasa to Kuta will mean changing buses in both Padangbai and Ubud and travelling via Sanur, for example. You'll need to book a day ahead, and discounts are offered it you book a second trip. Prices and timetables are available at www.peramatour. com.

By Car

The best way to really explore Bali is by car. You'll find car-rental agencies everywhere in Southern Bali offering competitive prices, and remember, everything is negotiable. You will need an International Drivers Permit (IDP), which is available from your local national motoring organisation, as well as your normal driver's licence.

However, before you rent it's worth keeping in mind that the traffic in Bali is chaotic at best, harrowing at worst. Driving is on the left-hand side, like Australia, but it can sometimes be hard to tell and I have never, ever seen an indicator being used. Other than people in front of

Watch where you walk

If you think driving in Bali can be fraught, so too can walking. Pedestrian crossings (zebra crossings) are largely ignored by motorists. Footpaths (sidewalks) as we know them rarely exist and you'll usually have to walk along the side of the road, so be mindful of cars and trucks as they whizz by. Even when footpaths do exist they are narrow—when two people pass each other one of them will have to step out into the traffic—or are blocked by parked cars or never-ending construction. They are also an up-and-down affair, with raised storm drains every few metres, although in many cases the cover is broken or missing and it is just a big gaping hole. Call me superstitious, but I just can't bring myself to step on any that are cracked—so many have fallen through that I'm sure one will collapse just when I step on it. If you are pushing a pram or in a wheelchair, you have no option but to use the road.

you having the right of way (drivers won't check for traffic when pulling out or making a turn, but they do listen for a horn), Bali doesn't seem to have any road rules as far as I can tell, although as a tourist you'll probably spend half your time on the side of the road arguing with traffic police over some trumped-up traffic infringement. Parking is a nightmare, good road maps are hard to find and signposting practically nonexistent. The Balinese also have a novel approach to determining who is at fault in the event of a crash: quite simply, as a foreigner the accident is *always* your fault. It's justified by the concept that if you had not been here, the accident would not have happened.

Consider instead hiring a car and driver. It usually only costs a few dollars more and is stress free—you are in Bali to relax after all. Your hotel can arrange this, although it will be much cheaper if you arrange it yourself at one of the transport/tour shops and kiosks you'll see everywhere, or simply negotiate a price with one of the hundreds of

people who will offer you 'transport' wherever you go.

By Motorbike

Hiring a motorbike or scooter is very popular in and around Kuta, and if you are game, can be a great way to get around, costing only a few dollars a day. You can even hire bikes with a rack for your surfboard.

If you have a motorbike licence already, get your IDP endorsed for motorbikes; otherwise, you'll need to get a local licence (requiring a written test but no road test), despite assurances from the guy you are hiring the bike from that you don't need one. Plenty of people hire a bike or scooter without a licence and you'll seldom be asked to produce one when you do the deal. You will by the police though, and if you have an accident, your travel insurance won't cover you without a valid licence.

Technically it is illegal to ride without a helmet, although you rarely see them worn, even by young school children, who are too young to ride a motorbike (but they do). As a foreigner though, you're more likely to get pulled over by police hoping to make a little extra money.

By Taxi

In Southern Bali taxis are a great way to get around, and relatively cheap compared to what you pay at home, although they are virtually nonexistent in Ubud and north of Sanur (although you'll find plenty of people offering transport in private cars). Many taxi drivers will even wait at no extra charge while you visit a temple or have a meal, something that can be useful in out of the way places such as Ulu Watu or Tanah Lot. Not all taxis are metered, so if you do flag down a taxi without

one, negotiate a price first. The best taxis are the blue Bluebird Taxis, **Bali Taxi** (☎ (0361) 701 111), which are always metered and have a good reputation for taking you where you want to go by the most direct route.

If you don't mind riding a short way without a helmet (not that the distance travelled makes any difference if you fall off and hit your head), the ubiquitous *ojek* (motorbike taxis) can be a cheap quick way to get around for short distances of just a kilometre or two. You can buy helmets (many with Viking horns attached) at souvenir shops and markets in and around Kuta, but they are probably not that useful in a crash.

Fast **Facts**

ATMS ATMs are everywhere in tourist areas and most use global networks, such as Cirrus and PLUS, and will accept international ATM cards and give cash advances on credit cards. Best ones to use are those attached to banks, rather than convenience stores. Beware, however, of fees imposed by your bank each time you use one. A trap for the unwary, especially if you are accustomed to using Australian ATMs that return your card before they give you the cash, is that most ATMS in Bali will spit out the cash, the receipt and then finally the card. Believe me, it can be very easy to walk away leaving your card in the ATM (I know from bitter experience!).

BABYSITTING Most hotels can arrange a babysitting service, and many have specialised kids clubs.

BUSINESS & SHOP HOURS Banks are open from 8am to 3 pm Monday to Friday, and 8am to 11am on Saturday. Government agencies operate from 8am to 3pm Monday to Thursday, 8am to noon on Friday. Shops in tourist areas are usually open from 9am or 10am to around 7pm or 8pm daily.

CLIMATE See Weather, earlier in this chapter.

CONSULATES & EMBASSIES
Australia: Jl Tantular 32, Renon, Denpasar (☎ (0361) 241 118; Monday to Friday 8am to noon and 12.30pm to 4pm). The Australian consulate also assists nationals of Canada and New Zealand. **UK:** Tirtra Nadi 20, Sanur (☎ (0361) 270 601; Monday to Thursday 8.30am to 12.30pm, Friday 11.30am to 6.30pm). **US:** Jl Hayam Wuruk 310, Denpasar (☎ (0361) 233 605; Monday to Friday 8am to 4.30pm).

CREDIT CARDS Credit cards are not universally accepted, even in tourist areas, so always ask before you order or strike a bargain. Where they are accepted, it's almost always Visa and MasterCard; American Express is less common and Diners Club and Discover are not used. Many businesses will add a surcharge on credit card purchases. Even if you have been quoted a price in US dollars (such as a tour or hotel room), it will be converted into rupiah when you present your credit card: Indonesian banking law does not permit credit card transactions in any other currency. Always carry cash and try to have smaller denominations if possible; many vendors cannot give change for a 100 000Rp note.

CUSTOMS Adults can bring in up to 200 cigarettes (or 50 cigars or 100g of other tobacco products) and 1 litre of alcohol. You can bring in as much foreign currency as you wish, but you are only allowed to bring in, or leave with, five million rupiah (around A$600). It is illegal to bring in any fresh fruit, pornography of any kind, weapons or drugs. Bali imposes strict sentences, including the death penalty, on anyone caught with even a small amount of illicit drugs (including cannabis or even just one ecstasy tablet), either at customs or on the street.

DENTISTS See Emergencies.

DOCTORS See Emergencies.

ELECTRICITY The current is 220 to 240 volts AC, 50 hertz. Sockets take two round pins, so you'll need a European adaptor.

EMBASSIES See Consulates & Embassies.

EMERGENCIES The emergency response centre coordinates all government services: dial ☎ 112. If you just need the **police**, dial ☎ 110; **ambulance** ☎ 118; **fire** ☎ 113. Most tourist areas have at least one or two health clinics, otherwise ask your hotel to recommend a doctor or dentist. If it's serious, the 24-hour **BIMC Hospital** (☎ (0361) 761 263; www.bimcbali. com) on Jl Ngurah Rai near Kuta has an emergency treatment room and can arrange medical evacuations. Even if you have travel insurance, most clinics and hospitals will require payment in advance.

FAMILY TRAVEL To locate accommodation, restaurants and attractions that are particularly kid-friendly, refer to the 'Kids' icon throughout this guide. Most Bali hotels accommodate families; all but the most expensive restaurants welcome children, although not all offer specific children's menus or high chairs.

GAY & LESBIAN TRAVELLERS Bali is quite gay friendly, although overt demonstrations of gay affection are not always tolerated in public. Gay and lesbian travellers will find it easy enough to rent a room with a double bed, but there are few, if any, exclusively gay clubs or bars. The *Bali Pink Pages,* published by the Bali Gay & Lesbian Association (www.balipinkpages.com) is your best bet for information on gay-friendly businesses and events.

HOLIDAYS Everything (except hospitals) is closed on Nyepi (see Festivals and Special Events). Other public holidays include New Year's Day (January 1), Chinese New Year (mid-February), Maulid or Mohammed's birthday (March/April/May), Good Friday (March/April), Buddha's birthday (April/May), Ascension Day (April/May), Indonesia Independence Day (August 17), Eid or the end of Ramadan (November/December), Christmas (December 25) and Islamic New Year. Banks and businesses are closed, but larger stores and some tourist attractions may remain open.

INSURANCE Travel insurance is a must for Bali. Check that your policy has adequate cover, including evacuation. If planning on hiring a car or motorbike, check the fine print—even if you get a local licence, you may not be covered. Some policies also don't cover scuba diving. Keep a copy of your insurance company's 24-hour helpline in your wallet.

INTERNET CAFES There's no shortage of internet cafes in Southern Bali, and anywhere tourists go. Rates are cheap, but connections can be a bit on the slow side, although things are improving. Many cafes and hotels also offer free wi-fi for paying customers, sometimes where you least expect it.

MAIL & POSTAGE Sending postcards and letters home from Bali is cheap, but slow. To send a postcard to Australia, the UK or US will cost less than US$1, but will take will take up to three weeks to get there. If you want to send home some surplus shopping, anything that weighs over 20g will be charged by weight. You can send parcels of up to 20kg. If you need something sent to you, you can pick it up at the post office in Kuta (Jl Selamet; Monday to Thursday 7am to 2pm, Friday 7am to 11am, Saturday 7am to 1pm) or Ubud (Jl Jembawan; daily 8am to 5pm).

Mail should be addressed to you with your surname in capital letters and underlined, and marked 'Kantor Pos'. If you know where you are staying, it might be easier to have mail sent to your hotel, but keep in mind that it will take two to three weeks to arrive from overseas.

MONEY Indonesia's unit of currency is the rupiah (Rp). You will occasionally see coins in denominations of 50, 100, 500 and 1000, but the smaller ones are not always available, so don't be surprised if you are frequently short-changed by a few hundred rupiah. Notes come in denominations of 1000, 5000, 10 000, 20 000, 50 000 and 100 000. The latter two can be hard to change, so try and collect as many of the smaller notes as you can. Most major bank branches offer currency exchange services and you'll find moneychangers on every street in busy tourist areas, where you'll usually get a better rate. Moneychangers advertise their daily exchange rates on billboards outside their shops, so look around. Use only 'authorised' moneychangers. Those with the higher rates usually charge a commission, so always ask first. Sometimes you'll get a different rate for higher denomination bills, such as 50s and 100s, so it's actually better to arrive with larger bills from home rather than a bundle of 5s and 10s. Most charge extra to change travellers cheques. Always count your money carefully in front of the moneychanger and double check their calculations (all those zeros can be bamboozling); being short-changed by shifty moneychangers is a common scam.

PASSPORTS & VISAS See Visas earlier in this chapter.

PHARMACIES Called *apoteks,* most tourist areas have at least one or two pharmacies, although they stock mostly local medicines. You can also buy common over-the-counter medications such as headache tablets and cough syrup at convenience stores. If you need to take regular medicine, carry enough medication with you for your trip and carry a copy of your prescription and a letter from your doctor detailing what the drugs are for.

SAFETY Compared to many places in Southeast Asia, Bali is a safe destination. Unfortunate terrorism attacks in the past aside, violent crime is fairly rare (apart from drunken yobbos on holidays beating each other up outside Kuta nightclubs), as is theft (if you don't consider being short-changed by moneychangers as theft or any crimes perpetrated by monkeys). However, it does pay to be careful and use common sense. Keep your wallet hidden, don't wear money belts or bum packs (fanny packs) outside your clothing and always keep your passport locked in a hotel safe. Always lock your hotel room and secure your bathroom door— thieves have been known to enter via open-air bathrooms. Be careful, especially at night, in and around Kuta, and never, ever leave your belongings unattended on the beach, particularly in Kuta. For most visitors to Bali, the most dangerous things encountered are the surf, the traffic and passive cigarette smoke (see below).

SMOKING Bali is one of the last outposts that is smoker-friendly. In other words, everywhere you go, from hotel lobbies to bars, restaurants and even buses, you'll find people merrily puffing away. Some hotels will offer nonsmoking rooms, but very few restaurants feature a nonsmoking section.

TAXES All accommodation has a combined tax and service charge of 21 per cent. Sometimes this is added to your bill or sometimes it's included in the quoted price, so always ask when comparing hotel prices. Restaurants and bars also charge a sales tax (and often a service charge as well) and it can range from 10, 15 or even 21 per cent. As a general rule of thumb, the fancier the restaurant, the higher the tax.

The tax, at whatever rate it is, is sometimes included in the price, sometimes not. Or it mightn't be charged at all.

A departure tax of 150000Rp is payable by all travellers upon leaving Bali, and is payable at the airport.

TAXIS See Getting Around.

TELEPHONES To make **international calls** from Bali, dial 011 and then the country code (Australia: 61, New Zealand: 64, US or Canada: 1, UK: 44, Ireland: 353), then the area code (dropping the first zero if applicable) and number. If using a mobile phone, you don't need to dial 011 but you will need to include the + sign before the number. For an **international operator**, dial ☎ 101. For **directory assistance**, dial ☎ 108. If calling from overseas, the international calling code for Indonesia is 62.

Bali has six telephone area codes, all beginning with 036. If you are calling Bali from another country, you will need to drop the 0 (eg, 62 361 XXX XXX), but if you are calling within Indonesia, you would simply dial 0361 XXX XXX. Mobile phone numbers begin with 08.

TIME Bali is eight hours ahead of Greenwich Mean Time, except during daylight saving time. That's two hours behind Eastern Standard Time in Australia, and 13 hours ahead of Eastern Standard Time in the US. Bali does not have daylight saving time in summer.

TIPPING Tipping is not expected anywhere, but is certainly appreciated. In restaurants and bars and even hotels it's not necessary to leave a tip if a service charge is included in the bill. Many guides at temples and other tourist attractions, and airport porters, work solely for tips. Most people round up taxi fares to the nearest 1000Rp, and it's appreciated if you tip drivers and massage therapists a few thousand rupiah.

TOURIST OFFICES   See Government Tourist Offices.

TOURIST TRAPS   A common con in tourist areas, particularly Kuta, is a version of a timeshare scam. It begins with a friendly local, often in an official-looking uniform, asking if you speak English and then wondering if you would like to either participate in a survey or, more frequently, offering you a 'scratch and win' ticket where you are invariably the lucky winner of a free holiday or some other great prize. The catch is that you have to attend a 'short'

holiday resort presentation to claim your 'prize'. Despite the offer of free transport to get you there and back, it will be a long and high-pressured sales pitch. Timeshare is a completely unregulated industry in Indonesia and if you do buy the 'holiday club' product, chances are you will certainly regret it.

TRAVELLERS WITH DISABILITIES
Sadly, Bali is not very user friendly when it comes to travellers with disabilities. Very few hotels, stores, attractions and toilets in Bali have wheelchair access. The same goes for transport options. Forget about navigating footpaths in a wheelchair, you'll need to fight for space on the road with all the other traffic.

Bali: **A Brief History**

7TH CENTURY Indian traders bring Hinduism to Bali.

MID-11TH CENTURY Java begins to have influence over Bali but remains, more or less semi-independent.

1284 Bali is conquered by Javanese ruler, King Kertanagara.

1292 Bali gains independence from Java with the death of King Kertanagara.

1343 Bali is conquered by East Java under the Hindu Majapahit kingdom, resulting in massive changes in Balinese society, including the introduction of the caste system. Those that did not like the changes fled to the hills and become known as Bali Aga ('original Balinese'). They still live separately in villages like Tenganan near Candidasa and maintain their ancient laws and traditions.

1520 The spread of Islam across Java is complete. Bali remains an isolated island outpost of Hinduism.

1546 The first of the sea temples (Pura Tanah Lot, Puru Ulu Watu) are built by Hindu priest Nirartha.

1597 Dutch explorer Cornelis de Houtman is one of the first Europeans to arrive in Bali, near modern-day Kuta.

1710 The Royal court is moved to Klungkung (now called Semarapura). Meanwhile, Dutch influence strengthens.

1846 The Dutch land military forces in Northern Bali and begin pitching various distrustful Balinese kingdoms against each other.

1890S The Dutch exploit struggles between rival Balinese kingdoms in the island's south and now effectively control the island.

1894 The Dutch take control over neighbouring Lombok.

1906 A dispute over the spoils of a wrecked ship escalates into a pitched battle at Sanur, in which the outclassed royal family and their followers fight a suicidal *puputan* (fight to the death) rather than face the ignominy of defeat. An estimated 1000 Balinese march to their death against the Dutch and their modern weapons.

1908 A similar massacre occurs in Klungkung, this time 4000 Balinese are killed.

1930S Western artists such as Walter Spies, composers like Colin McPhee and anthropologist Margaret Mead start singing the praises of Balinese beauty and culture to the rest of the world. Spies co-founds the Pita Maha artists' cooperative in Ubud, giving rise to the Young Artists Movement. Bob and Louise Koke build a couple of bungalows on deserted Kuta beach, name them the Kuta Beach Hotel and welcome their first guests.

1942 Japanese forces land at Sanur and soon occupy the entire island.

AUGUST, 1945 Japanese surrender marks the end of WWII. Sukarno proclaims Indonesian Independence on August 17, although the Dutch are not convinced.

NOVEMBER 20, 1946 Freedom fighter Gusti Ngurah Rai dies, along with his entire fighting force, in a suicide attack in central Bali known as the Battle of Marga.

DECEMBER 29, 1949 The Dutch formally recognise Indonesian independence, although Indonesians celebrate Independence Day as August 17, 1945.

1963 Bali's highest and most holy volcano erupts, killing thousands, and leaving hundreds of thousands homeless.

1965–6 Attempted Communist coup leads to fall of Sukarno and rise of Suharto. Anti-communist purges result in the death of somewhere between 50 and 100 Balinese.

1970S Surfers discover the delights of Bali's beaches, followed by backpackers and ultimately more mainstream tourists. Kuta will never be the same again.

OCTOBER 12, 2002 Militant Islamists explode two bombs in two nightclubs on busy Jl Legian in Kuta, killing at least 202 people, mostly foreigners.

OCTOBER 1, 2005 Three suicide bombers blow themselves up; one in Kuta Square, the other two at seafood cafes on Jimbaran Beach. Twenty people die, 15 of them Balinese. Bali's economy suffers as tourists stay away in droves.

2009 Bali's tourist numbers hit record highs as the Balinese joyfully welcome more than two million visitors throughout the year.

Useful Phrases

Almost everyone in tourist-oriented Bali speaks some English, so you can easily get by without knowing any Bahasa Indonesia at all. Learn a few words though, and you'll be sure to earn a smile, if not some new friends.

Greetings & Conversation Starters

Good morning	*Selamat pagi*
Good afternoon	*Selamat siang*
Good evening	*Selamat sore*
Goodnight	*Selamat malam*
Goodbye (said to people leaving)	*Selamat jalan*
Goodbye (said to people staying)	*Selamat tinggal*
How are you?	*Apa kabar?*
I am fine	*Kabar baik*
What is your name?	*Siapa nama anda?*
My name is…	*Nama saya…*
Nice to meet you	*Senang berkenalan dengan anda*
See you later	*Sampai jumpa lagi*
I do not understand	*Saya tidak mengerti*
I do not speak Indonesian	*Saya tidak mengerti bahasa*

General

Yes	*Ya/Tentu*
OK	*Beres*
No/not	*Tidak bukan*
Thank you	*Terima kasih*
You're welcome	*Kembali*
Please	*Tolong/Silakan*
Excuse me	*Permisi*
Sorry	*Ma'af*
What time is it?	*Jam berapa?*
Please help me!	*Tolonglah saya!*
Call a doctor!	*Panggil dokter!*
Call the police!	*Panggil polisi!*

Questions You'll Be Asked

Dari mana?	Where have you just come from?
Tuan asal dari mana?	What country are you from?
Mau ke mana?	Where are you going?

Shopping

Only looking	*Lihat saja*
I want to buy this	*Saya mau beli*
How much?	*Berapa?*
Expensive	*Mahal*
Can you make it cheaper?	*Boleh kurang harganya?*
What is your fixed price?	*Harga pas berapa?*
Will you please leave me alone?	*Sudikah anda membiarkan saya sendiri?*

Eating

What would you like to drink?	*Tuan mau minum apa?*
What would you like to eat?	*Tuan mau makan apa?*
I want the menu please	*Saya mau daftar makanan minta*
I would like to drink water/beer	*Mau minum air/bir*
Drinking water	*Air minum*
(Hot) Tea/coffee	*Teh (panas)/kopi*
Without sugar/milk	*Tanpa gula/susu*
With sugar/milk	*Sedikit gula/susu*
How do you say it in English?	*Apa bahasa Inggrisnya (while pointing)?*
The bill (cheque) please	*Tolong bonnya*

Accommodation

The best hotel	*Hotel paling baik*
The cheapest hotel	*Hotel paling murah*
Clean	*Bersih*
Are there rooms available?	*Ada Kamar?*
Do you have any air-conditioned rooms?	*Ada kamar dengan AC?*
Fan	*Kipas*
What is the cost of the room?	*Berapa ongkos kamar?*
Two people	*Dua orang*
Is there a toilet, bathroom?	*Ada WC, tempat mandi?*
Bedsheet	*Sprei*
Blanket	*Selimut*
Towel	*Handuk*
Soap	*Sabun*
Can you wash clothes?	*Bisa cuci pakaian?*

Transport

Where is the bus station?	*Stasiun bis dimana?*
When is there a bus to ...?	*Kapan ada bis ke ...?*
What time does it leave?	*Berangkat jam berapa?*
How many hours to ...?	*Beraoa jam sampai ...?*

Directions

Where is ...?	*Dimana ...?*
Where is the toilet?	*Dimana kamar kecil?*
Where is the beach?	*Dimana pantai?*
Where is there a hotel?	*Mana ada hotel?*
Where is there a restaurant?	*Mana ada rumah makan?*
How far is it?	*Berapa jauh dari sini?*
What is the name of this street?	*Apa nama jalan ini?*
I'm lost	*Saya tersesat*

Understanding Directions

Near	*Dekat*
Far	*Jauh*
North	*Utara*
South	*Selatan*
East	*Timur*

West	Barat
Right	Kanan
Left	Kiri

Days of the Week

Sunday	Minggu
Monday	Senin
Tuesday	Selasa
Wednesday	Rabu
Thursday	Kamis
Friday	Jum'at
Saturday	Sabtu
Yesterday	Kemarin
Today	Hari ini
Tomorrow	Besok
Day after tomorrow	Lusa

Time

Day	Hari
Week	Minggu
Month	Bulan
Year	Tahun

Numbers

0	Nol
1	Satu
2	Dua
3	Tiga
4	Empat
5	Lima
6	Enam
7	Tujuh
8	Delapan
9	Sembilan
10	Sepulah
11	Sebalas
100	Seratus
1000	Seribu
10	Sepuluh ribu
1	Sejuta

Once you've mastered one to 10, you can add the following suffixes:

Teens	Belas
12	Dua belas
13	Tiga belas
14	Empat belas
15	Lima belas
Tens	Puluh
20	Dua puluh
25	Dua puluh lima
30	Tiga puluh
40	Empat puluh

Hundreds	Ratus
200	Dua ratus
500	Lima ratus
Thousands	Ribu
Millions	Juta

Phone Numbers & Websites

Airlines

AIR ASIA
☎ 021 5050 5058
www.airasia.com

CATHAY PACIFIC
☎ 0804 188 8888 by landline
☎ 021 515 1747 by mobile phone
www.cathaypacific.com

CHINA AIRLINES
☎ (0361) 757 298
www.china-airlines.com

EVA AIR
☎ (0361) 759 773
www.evaair.com

GARUDA INDONESIA
☎ (0361) 225 320 in Bali
☎ 1300 365 330 in Australia
www.garuda-indonesia.com

JAPAN AIRLINES
☎ (0361) 757 077
www.jal.com

JETSTAR
☎ +613/9347 0153 from Bali
☎ 131 538 in Australia
www.jetstar.com

KOREAN AIR
☎ (0361) 768 377
www.koreanair.com

LION AIR
☎ (0361) 765 183
www2.lionair.id

MALAYSIA AIRLINES
☎ (0361) 764 995
www.malaysiaairlines.com

PACIFIC BLUE
☎ +617/3295 2284 from Bali
☎ 131 645 in Australia
www.flypacificblue.com

QATAR AIRWAYS
☎ (0361) 752 222
www.qatarairways.com

SINGAPORE AIRLINES
☎ (0361) 768 3888
www.singaporeair.com

THAI AIRWAYS
☎ (0361) 288 141
www.thaiair.com

Index

See also Accommodation and Restaurant indexes, below.

A

Accommodation, 100–114.
   See also Accommodation Index
      best, 100
      prices, 106
Addresses, finding, 166
Agung Rai Museum of Art (ARMA; Ubud), 33, 71, 142
Air Panas Banjar, 81
Air Terjun Gitgit, 80
Air travel, 165
Anturan, 81, 88
Architecture, 3–4
ARMA (Agung Rai Museum of Art; Ubud), 33, 71
Art and artists, 31–33
Art and handicrafts, shopping for, 142–144
Art galleries, 142–144
   Seminyak, 55–57
   Ubud, 18, 31
Art museums
   Agung Rai Museum of Art (ARMA; Ubud), 33, 71
   Blanco Renaissance Museum (Ubud), 18, 32, 69
   Museum Le Mayeur (Sanur), 17, 33
   Museum Negri Propinsi Bali (Denpasar), 82
   Museum Puri Lukisan (Ubud), 32
   Neka Art Museum (near Ubud), 14, 31, 69
   Pasifika Museum (Nusa Dua), 21, 33, 61
   Seniwati (Ubud), 18, 32
Art Zoo (Ubud), 31
Ashitaba (Seminyak), 148
ATMs (automated-teller machines), 168
Australia, embassy and consulate, 168
Ayam betutu (smoked duck or chicken), 48
Ayana's Spa on the Rocks (Ayana Resort and Spa), 41
Ayung River, 98

B

Babi guling (suckling pig), 48
Babysitting, 168
Bahiana (Seminyak), 158
Bali Advertiser, 162
Bali Aga people, 76
Bali Arts Festival, 163
Bali Bird Park (near Ubud), 28
Bali Collection (Nusa Dua), 62
Bali Galleria (Kuta), 147
Bali High, 73
Bali Kite Festival, 163
Bali Kitesurfing School (Sanur), 98
Balinese dance and music, 156
Balinese New Year, 162
Bali Pink Pages, 169
Bali Safari & Marine Park, 28
Bali Taxi, 168
Banana boats, 97
Bargaining, 5, 10, 144
Barong dance, 157
Baskets, 145
Bat Cave Temple (Pura Goa Lawah), 77
Batik (Batubulan), 142–143
Batubulan, 73
Beaches, 86–90. *See also* specific beaches
   best, 86
Beach Market (Sanur), 65
Beach Promenade (Sanur), 65
Beachwear, shopping for, 145
Bebek (smoked duck or chicken), 48
Bedugul Botanic Gardens (Candikuning), 93
Bemo Corner (Kuta), 52
Bemo (minibus), 166
Benoa, 63
Biking, 93
Bingtang beer, 5
Bird-watching, Bali Bird Park (near Ubud), 28
Blanco, Antonio, 32
Blanco Renaissance Museum (Ubud), 18, 32, 69
Blue Glue (Seminyak), 145
Bonnet, Rudolf, 31, 32
Bonsai garden (Jl Danau Tamblingan), 18
Books on Bali, 164
Bookstores, 146–147
Botanic Garden (near Ubud), 18, 45, 70–71
Bounty (Kuta), 158
Brahma Vihara Arama, 81

Braids, 27
Bubur Injin, 48
Bukit Peninsula, 59–63
Bumbu Bali Cooking School
   Sanur, 48
   Ubud, 19, 48
Bungy jumping, 93
Business and shop hours, 168
Bus travel, 166

C

Café Lotus (Ubud), 156
Candidasa, 22, 76
   beach, 88
Car rentals, 166
Car travel, 10, 166–167
Cell phones, 164
Celuk, 24, 73
Children, families with, 26–29, 169
Chinese temple (Benoa), 63
Chinese temple (Kuta), 52
Climate, 163
Clothing and accessories, 145–146
Coffee, Kopi Luwak (cat-poo coffee), 5, 48
   Sai Land Coffee Plantation (Taman), 73
Conrad Bali, wedding chapel, 41
Consulates, 168
Cooking schools, 48
   Bumbu Bali Cooking School (Ubud), 19
Couples massage, 41
Credit cards, 169
Cremation ceremonies, 37–38
Currency and currency exchange, 170
Customs regulations, 169

D

Danau Bratan, 79
Dance clubs, 158–160
Dances, traditional, 157
Dari Bali (Ubud), 145
Day of Silence (Nyepi), 162–163
Denpasar, 82
Denpasar airport (Ngurah Rai Airport), 165
Dentists, 169
Department stores and malls, 147–148
Dining, 4, 116–136. *See also* Restaurant Index
   best, 116

Disabilities, travellers with, 172
Discovery Mall (Tuban), 147–148
Doctors, 169
Dolphin Family (Ubud), 143
Double Six Beach, 53
Double Six (Kuta), 158
Downhill, Bali Bike Baik Tours, 93
Downhill cycling, 93
Dreamland, 90
Drifter (Seminyak), 145

E
Eastern Bali, 74–77
Elephant Cave (Goa Gajah; Ubud), 13, 19, 71
Elephant Safari Park (near Ubud), 29
Elephant trekking, 93
Embassies, 168
Emergencies, 169

F
Fabrics, 147
Families with children, 26–29, 169
Ferries, 165
Festivals and special events, 162–163
Fire and Trance Dance (Kecak), 5–6, 14, 157
Fishing, 97
Fishing boats
Kedonganan Beach, 59
Sanur, 66
Fish markets, Jimbaran, 13, 59
Fish Spa (Seminyak), 44
Flying Dragon (Ubud), 150
Food and cuisine, 47–48.
See also Markets;
Restaurants
cooking schools, 48
Food stalls (warungs), 4

G
Gajah Mas Gallery (Ubud), 143
Galungan Ceremony, 162
Ganesha Bookshop (Ubud), 146
Ganesha Gallery (Sayan), 61
Gangs (Kuta), 51
Gardens at Bali Hyatt (Sanur), 66
Gays and lesbians, 169

Gitgit waterfalls, 79–80
Goa Gajah (Elephant Cave; Ubud), 13, 19, 71
Government tourist offices, 162
Gudang Keramik (Sanur), 66
Gunung Agung, 23, 39, 75
climbing, 95
Gunung Batur, climbing, 95

H
Hard Rock Cafe (Kuta), 159
Harmonis (Ubud), 145
Haveli (Seminyak), 148
High season, 162
Hiking and walking, 95, 167
Holidays, 169–170
Homewares, 148
Honeymoons, 41
Horseback riding, 93
Hospital, 169
Hotels, 100–114. See also
Accommodation Index
best, 100
prices, 106
Hot springs, 6
Air Panas Banjar, 81
Hu'u (Seminyak), 156

I
Icon Asian Arts (Seminyak), 55
Impossibles, 90
Insurance, 170
Internet access, 170
InTouch U.S.A., 164

J
Jalan Oberoi (Seminyak), 55
Jalan Raya Seminyak, 56–57
Jalan Raya Ubud, 69
Jamu Spa (Sanur), 18, 67
Jamu Spa School (Tuban), 44
Jari Menari (Seminyak), 43–44, 56
Jazz Cafe (Ubud), 159
Jewellery, 148–149
Jimbaran Bay, 61
Jimbaran Beach, 13, 21, 41, 59–61, 88
fish markets, 13
surfing, 90
Jl Hanoman (Ubud), 14, 19
Jl Raya Ubud (Ubud), 19
Jl Wenara Wana (Monkey Forest Road; Ubud), 14, 19, 70

K
Kalibukbuk, 81
beach, 88–89
Kampung Arab (Denpasar), 84
Kecak (Fire and Trance Dance), 5–6, 14, 157
Ubud, 71
Kenko Reflexology (Legian), 43
Kids, 26–29, 169
Kintamani, 73
Kite Festival (Sanur), 28
Kite flying
Bali Kite Festival, 163
Sanur, 28, 67
Kite surfing, 98
Sanur, 65–66
Klungkung (Semarapura), 74–75
Koke, Robert A, 31
Kopi Luwak (cat-poo coffee), 5, 48
Sai Land Coffee Plantation (Taman), 73
Ku De Ta (Seminyak), 15, 157
Kuningan Ceremony, 162
Kupu Kupu Gallery (Ubud), 143
Kuta Karnival, 163
Kuta/Kuta Beach, 15, 17, 51–53, 89
braids, 27
massage on, 43
surfing, 27–28, 90
Kuta Square, 52

L
Legian, 51–53
beach, 53, 89
Legong dance, 157
Le Mayeur, Adrien, 17, 65
Lempad, I Gusti Nyoman, 31
Liberty, USS (wreck), 98
Light Spirit (Ubud), 45
Live music and dance clubs, 158–160
Lodging, 100–114. See also
Accommodation Index
best, 100
prices, 106
Lovina, 23, 79, 81
Lucy's Batik (Seminyak), 147
Lulu Yasmine (Seminyak), 145

M
Macan Tiger (Ubud), 143
Maha Blanco Jewellery (Ubud), 148
Mail and postage, 170

Mangku Made Gina (Ubud), 143–144
Markets, 149
  Denpasar, 84
  Jimbaran, 60
  Kuta, 52
  Seminyak, 56
Mas, 73
Massages, 43–45. *See also* Spas
  for couples, 41
  sound, 45
Matahari (Kuta), 147
Medewi, surfing, 90
Meditation, 45
Memorial Wall (Legian), 53
Mengwi, 36
Migliavacca, Milo, 145
Milo's Bazaar (Seminyak), 145
Minibus (bemo), 166
Miracle Massage (Kuta), 52
Moari shopping (Ubud), 150
Mobile phones, 164
Monkey Forest Rd (Jl Wenara Wana; Ubud), 14, 19, 70
Monkeys, 5, 79
Morena (Seminyak), 146
Motorbikes, 167–168
Museum Buleleng (Gitgit), 80
Museum Le Mayeur (Sanur), 17, 33, 65
Museum Negri Propinsi Bali (State Museum; Denpasar), 33, 82
Museum Puri Lukisan (Ubud), 32
Music and instruments, 150

N

Nasi campur, 47
Nasi goreng, 47
Neka Art Museum (near Ubud), 14, 18, 31, 69
New Queen Pub & Restaurant (Candidasa), 160
New Year, Balinese, 162
Ngurah Rai Airport (Denpasar airport), 165
Nightlife and entertainment, 152–160
  Balinese dance and music, 156
  bars and lounges, 156–158
  best bets, 152
  live music and dance clubs, 158–160

Nogo Bali Ikat Centre (Sanur), 66–67
Northern Bali, 79–84
Nusa Dua, 21
  beach, 89
  surfing, 90
Nusa Dua Beach Promenade, 62
Nyepi (Day of Silence), 162–163

O

Oceans 27 (Tuban), 157
Ogoh-ogoh, 163
Outdoor activities, 92–98

P

Paddle surfing, 97
Parasailing, 97
Pasar Anyar (Singaraja), 80
Pasar Badung (Denpasar), 47, 84, 147
Pasar Kumbasari (Denpasar), 84, 150
Pasar Sari Meta Nadi (Legian), 149
Pasar Ubud, 149
Pasifika Museum (Nusa Dua), 21, 33, 61
Pasir Putih, 76
Paul Ropp (Seminyak), 55–56, 146
Paul's Place (Seminyak), 146
Perama tourist shuttle bus, 166
Periplus (Tuban, Ubud), 146–147
Pharmacies, 170
Pita Maha artists' cooperative (Ubud), 31–33
Politeness, 10
Pondok Bamboo Music Shop (Ubud), 150
Poppies Lane (Kuta), 52–53
Postage, 170
Produce markets, 149
  Denpasar, 84
  Jimbaran, 60
  Kuta, 52
  Pasar Badung (Denpasar), 84
  Seminyak, 56
  Singaraja, 80
Pro Surf School (Kuta), 28
Pulau Menjangan, 98
Puputan Square (Denpasar), 83
Pura Batu Karu (Ubud), 156
Pura Batur, 38

Pura Besakih, 38–39, 75
Pura Dalem Ubud (Temple of the Dead), 19, 37–38, 156
Pura Goa Lawah (Bat Cave Temple), 77
Pura Jagatnatha (Denpasar), 39, 83
Pura Luhur Ulu Watu, 13, 35, 61, 156
Pura Maospahit (Denpasar), 84
Pura Petitenget (Seminyak), 55
Pura Taman Ayun (Mengwi), 36
Pura Taman Saraswati (Ubud), 19, 37
Pura Ulun Bratan, 79
Pura Ulun Siwi (Jimbaran), 59
Puri Pemecutan (Denpasar), 84

Q

Quiksilver Surf School (Kuta), 28

R

Rai Sandi (Ubud), 146
Reefs, 98
Reflexology treatments, 43, 52, 113
Religious processions, 6
Resorts and hotels, 100–114. *See also* Accommodation Index
  best, 100
  prices, 106
Restaurants, 4, 116–136. *See also* Restaurant Index
  best, 116
Rice paddies (rice paddy walks), 5, 14
  northern Bali, 79
  Ubud, 19, 69–70, 95
Rio Helmi (Ubud), 32
RoadPost, 164
The Rock Bar (Jimbaran), 158
Romantic Bali, 40–41
Ropp, Paul (Seminyak), 55–56

S

Sacred Monkey Forest Sanctuary (Ubud), 19, 29, 70
Safety, 171
Sai Land Coffee Plantation (Taman), 48
Sanghyang Widi, 39

Sanur, 17, 21, 65–67
  beach, 89
  kite flying, 28
  surfing, 90
Sari Amerta (Batubulan), 143
Sarongs, 10
Sate Bali (Seminyak), 48
Sate lilit, 47
Saya Gallery (Seminyak), 56
Scooters, 167–168
Scuba diving, 98
Seafood, 4, 13, 47, 60
Sea Gypsy (Seminyak), 148
Seasons, 162
Sei-Sui (Ubud), 146
Selandong, 39
Semarapura (Klungkung), 74–75
Seminyak, 17, 24, 54–57
  beach, 57, 90
  hiking from Tuban to, 95
  shopping, 15
  surfing, 90
Seminyak Square, 55
Seniwati (Ubud), 18, 32
Shibana (Seminyak), 146
Shopping, 138–150
  art and handicrafts, 142–144
  bargaining, 144
  beachwear, 145
  best, 138
  bookstores, 146–147
  clothing and accessories, 145–146
  department stores and malls, 147–148
  fabrics, 147
  homewares, 148
  markets, 149
  music and instruments, 150
  Seminyak, 15
  shop hours, 168
  souvenirs, 150
  yoga gear, 150
Sideman Road, 75
Sika Gallery (Ubud), 31
Silver, 24, 73
Silver (Celuk), 149
Singaraja, 80–81
Singaraja Museum & Library, 80
Singaraja Waterfront, 81
Sip Wine Bar (Seminyak), 157–158
sks (Seminyak), 146
Sky Garden Lounge (Kuta), 160
Smit, Arie, 31
Smoking, 171

Snorkeling, 98
Sobek Bali Utama, 98
Sound massage, 45
Souvenirs, 150
Spas, 42–45
  Jamu Spa (Sanur), 18
Spa treatments, 3
Special events and festivals, 162–163
Spies, Walter, 31–33
Spiritual places and experiences, 35–39
State Museum (Museum Negri Propinsi Bali; Denpasar), 33, 82
Stone Pillar (Sanur), 66
Strategies for seeing Bali, 9–10
Studio Perak (Ubud), 149
Sun exposure, 9
Sunset viewing, 4
Surfer Girl (Kuta), 145
Surfing, 4–5
  best breaks, 90
  kite, 98
  Kuta, 27–28
  paddle, 97
Surf schools, 15
Symon, 31–32

T

Taman, 73
Taman Ajung, 76
Taman Kertha Gosa (Semarapura), 21–22, 74
Taman Tirta Gangga, 23, 75–76
Tampaksiring, 73
Tanah Lot, 35–36
Tanda Mata (Ubud), 148
Tanjung Benoa (Nusa Dua), 63, 90
Taxes, 171
Taxis, 168
Tegun Folk Art Gallery (Ubud), 150
Telaga Waja River, 98
Telephones, 171
Temples, 3, 35–39. *See also specific temples*
  etiquette, 39
Tenganan, 22, 76–77
Theatre Art Gallery, 57
Threads of Life (Ubud), 147
Time zone, 171
Tipping, 171–172
Tjokorda Gede Agung Sukawati, 32
Toko East (Ubud), 148

Tourist offices, 162
Tourist shuttle, 166
Tourist traps, 172
Travelling to Bali, 165–166
Travel insurance, 170
Treetop Adventure Park (Candikuning), 93
Tropis Club (Lovina), 160
Tuban, 51
  hiking to Seminyak, 95
Tuban Beach, 90

U

Ubud, 14, 24, 69–71, 73
Ubud Palace, 19, 69, 156
Ubud Sari Health Resort, spa, 45
Ubud Writers & Readers Festival, 163
Ubud Yoga Centre, 44
Ulu Watu, 90
Uluwatu (Kuta), 144
Umalas Equestrian Resort (Kerobokan), 93
United Kingdom, embassy and consulate, 168
United States, embassy and consulate, 168
USS Liberty (wreck), 98

V

Vaikuntha Gallery (Seminyak), 56
Visas, 164
Visitor information, 162

W

Warung Rasta (Lovina), 160
Warungs (food stalls), 4
Warung Sunrise (Sanur), 160
Water, drinking, 9
Waterbom (Tuban), 27, 51
Watersports, 97–98
Wayan's Shop (Ubud), 145
Weather, 163
Websites, useful, 163–164
Weddings, 41
Wheelchair accessibility, 172
White-water rafting, 98
Wibisana (Seminyak), 148
Women, in temples, 39
Woodwork Market (Sanur), 66

Y

Yoga, Ubud, 44
The Yoga Shop (Ubud), 150
Young Artists Movement, 31
Yudha Mandala Tama (Singaraja), 80, 81

Accommodation

Abi Bali Villa (Jimbaran), 105
Alila Villas (Ulu Watu), 105
All Seasons (Legian), 105
Amandari (Ubud), 105–106
Amankila (Manggis), 41, 106
Amanusa (Nusa Dua), 106
Anantara (Seminyak), 107
Ayana Resort and Spa, 107
Bali Coconut Hotel (Legian), 107
Bali Hyatt (Sanur), 107
Bali Taman Resort & Spa (Lovina), 107–108
Banyan Tree Ungasan (Ulu Watu), 108
Best Western Resort (Kuta), 108–109
Club Med Bali (Nusa Dua), 109
Conrad Bali (Nusa Dua), 109
Hard Rock Hotel (Kuta), 109
InterContinental Bali Resort (Jimbaran), 109
Kamandalu (Ubud), 109
Laguna Resort & Spa (Nusa Dua), 110
Mercure Kuta Bali (Kuta), 110
Mercure Resort (Sanur), 110
Mutiara Bali Resort (Seminyak), 110
Nick's Pension (Ubud), 110–111
Novotel Bali Benoa (Tanjung Benoa), 111
Novotel Bali Nusa Dua, 111
Novus Bali Villas Resort & Spa (Seminyak), 111
Novus Taman Bebek Resort & Spa (Ubud), 111–112
The Oberoi (Seminyak), 112
The Pavilions (Sanur), 112
Pelangi Bali Hotel (Seminyak), 112
Pullman Bali Legian Nirwana (Legian), 112–113
Space at Bali (Legian), 113
Tandjung Sari (Sanur), 113
Uma (Ubud), 113–114
Villa Sasoon (Candidasa), 114
The Water Garden (Candidasa), 114
Westin Resort (Nusa Dua), 114

Restaurants

Anjani (Sanur), 123
Ayam Taliwanga (Kuta), 123
Balcony (Kuta), 123
Bali Baliku (Jimbaran), 123
Beach Cafe (Sanur), 123
Bebek Bengil (Ubud), 48, 123–124
Benny's Bistro (Seminyak), 124
Bintang Bali (Lovina), 124
Blue Ocean (Legian), 15, 124
Bonsai (Sanur), 124
Bumbu Bali (Tanjung Benoa), 125
Bumbu Bali (Ubud), 125
Café Bali (Seminyak), 125
Café Batu Jumbar (Sanur), 125
Café Lotus (Ubud), 125–126
Café Seminyak, 126
Casa Luna (Sanur), 126
Casa Luna (Ubud), 126
Charming (Sanur), 18, 126
Coco Bistro (Ubud), 126–127
Coriander (Sanur), 127
Dewi Sri (Tuban), 127
Fortuin (Jimbaran), 127
Gado Gado Kafe (Seminyak), 127
Ganesha Cafe (Jimbaran), 127–128
Goodys (Legian), 128
Gourmet Cafe (Seminyak), 128
Green Garden (Tuban), 128
Havana Club (Kuta), 128
Ibu Rai (Ubud), 128
Indo-National (Legian), 128
Kafe Batan Waru (Kuta & Ubud), 48, 128–129
Ketaput (Kuta), 129
Kopi Pot (Kuta), 129
Kori (Kuta), 129
Kunti II (Kuta), 129
Kunyit Bali (Tuban), 47, 129
La Lucciola (Seminyak), 130
Legong (Candidasa), 130
Lotus Seaview (Candidasa), 130
Made's Warung (Kuta), 47, 130
Mango Beach Bar (Sanur), 130
Mannekepis (Seminyak), 57, 130–131
Ming Le Resto (Sanur), 131
Mozaic (Ubud), 131
Mr Dolphin (Lovina), 131
Murni's Warung (Ubud), 131
Nelayan (Tanjung Benoa), 131
Nomad (Ubud), 132
Papa's (Legian), 132
Puri Garden (Ubud), 132–133
Puri Pandan (Candidasa), 132
Sanur Beach Market Restaurant, 132
Sari Bundo (Sanur), 133
Sarong (Seminyak), 133
Sate Bali (Seminyak), 133
Seaside (Legian), 133
Stiff Chilli (Sanur), 66, 133
Taman Curry Warung (Ubud), 133
Tao (Tanjung Benoa), 134
Teba Cafe (Jimbaran), 41, 47, 134
Terazo (Ubud), 134
Toke (Candidasa), 134
Trattoria (Seminyak), 135
The Tree (Tanjung Benoa), 134
Tropical (Ubud), 135
Tropis Club (Lovina), 135
Vincent's (Candidasa), 135
Warung Bamboo (Jimbaran), 135
Warung Bamboo (Lovina), 135
Warung Ibu Oka (Ubud), 14, 19, 48, 135–136
Warung Indonesia (Kuta), 136
Warung Nikmat (Kuta), 136
Yutz (Legian), 136

Photo **Credits**

Front cover/p. i: left: © Photolibrary / Novastock; centre: © Photolibrary / age fotostock; right: © Photolibrary / Lite Productions; back cover: © Alila Villas Uluwatu; p. ii, from top to bottom: © Andi Sucirta, © Andi Sucirta, © Andi Sucirta, © Lee Atkinson, © Andi Sucirta; p. iii, from top to bottom: © Lee Atkinson, © Andi Sucirta, © Alila Villas Uluwatu, © Sarong restaurant, © Lee Atkinson; p. viii, © Andi Sucirta; p. 3, top: © Uma Ubud; p. 3, bottom: © Lee Atkinson; p. 4, top: © Lee Atkinson; p. 4, bottom: © Lee Atkinson; p. 5, top: © Lee Atkinson; p. 5, bottom: © Andi Sucirta; p. 6, top: © Andi Sucirta; p. 6, bottom: © Lee Atkinson; p. 7: © Andi Sucirta; p. 9: © Andi Sucirta; p. 10: © Andi Sucirta; p. 11: © Andi Sucirta; p. 13: © Andi Sucirta; p. 14, top: © Andi Sucirta; p. 14, bottom: © Andi Sucirta; p. 15, top: © Andi Sucirta; p. 15, bottom: © Ku De Ta; p. 17: © Andi Sucirta; p. 18, top: © Andi Sucirta; p. 18, bottom: © Andi Sucirta; p. 19, top: © Lee Atkinson; p. 19, bottom: © Lee Atkinson; p. 21: © Lee Atkinson; p. 22, top: © Andi Sucirta; p. 22, bottom: © Andi Sucirta; p. 23, top: © Lee Atkinson; p. 23, bottom: © Andi Sucirta; p. 24: © Lee Atkinson; p. 25: © Lee Atkinson; p. 27: © Waterbom; p. 28, top: © Lee Atkinson; p. 28, bottom: © Lee Atkinson; p. 29: © Andi Sucirta; p. 31: © Lee Atkinson; p. 32: © Andi Sucirta; p. 33: © Lee Atkinson; p. 35: © Lee Atkinson; p. 36, top: © Andi Sucirta; p. 36, bottom: © Andi Sucirta; p. 37: © Lee Atkinson; p. 38, top: © Andi Sucirta; p. 38, bottom: © Lee Atkinson; p. 39: © Lee Atkinson; p. 41, top: © Amankila; p. 41, bottom: © Conrad Bali; p. 43: © Andi Sucirta; p. 44, top: © Andi Sucirta; p. 44, bottom: © Uma Ubud; p. 45: © Andi Sucirta; p. 47, top: © Brooke Lyons; p. 47, bottom: © Andi Sucirta; p. 48: © Andi Sucirta; p. 49: © Andi Sucirta; p. 51, top: © Andi Sucirta; p. 51, bottom: © Lee Atkinson; p. 52: © Lee Atkinson; p. 53, top: © Lee Atkinson; p. 53, bottom: © Andi Sucirta; p. 55, top: © Lee Atkinson; p. 55, bottom: © Icon Asian Arts; p. 56: © Lee Atkinson; p. 57, top: © Andi Sucirta; p. 57, bottom: © Ku De Ta; p. 59: © Lee Atkinson; p. 60: © Andi Sucirta; p. 61: Andi Sucirta; p. 62, top: © Andi Sucirta; p. 62, bottom: © Lee Atkinson; p. 63, top: © Lee Atkinson; p. 63, bottom: © Lee Atkinson; p. 65: © Lee Atkinson; p. 66, top: © Andi Sucirta; p. 66, bottom: © Andi Sucirta; p. 66, top: © Andi Sucirta; p. 66, bottom: © Andi Sucirta; p. 67, top: © Andi Sucirta; p. 67, centre: © Andi Sucirta; p. 67, bottom: © Lee Atkinson; p. 69: © Lee Atkinson; p. 70, top: © Lee Atkinson; p. 70, bottom: © Lee Atkinson; p. 71, top: © Lee Atkinson; p. 71, bottom: © Lee Atkinson; p. 73, top: © Lee Atkinson; p. 73, bottom: © Andi Sucirta; p. 74: © Lee Atkinson; p. 75, top: © Lee Atkinson; p. 75, bottom: © Lee Atkinson; p. 76, top © Andi Sucirta; p. 76, bottom: © Lee Atkinson; p. 77, top: © Lee Atkinson; p. 77, bottom: © Lee Atkinson; p. 79, top © Andi Sucirta; p. 79, bottom: © Lee Atkinson; p. 80, top © Andi Sucirta; p. 80, bottom: © Lee Atkinson; p. 81, top © Andi Sucirta; p. 81, bottom: © Lee Atkinson; p. 83, top © Andi Sucirta; p. 83, bottom: © Lee Atkinson; p. 84, top: © Lee Atkinson; p. 84, bottom: © Lee Atkinson; p. 85: © Lee Atkinson; p. 86: © Lee Atkinson; p. 88: © Lee Atkinson; p. 89, top: © Andi Sucirta; p. 89, bottom: © Accor Hotel Bali; p. 90, top: © Andi Sucirta; p. 90, bottom: © technotr; p. 91: © Andi Sucirta; p. 91: © Andi Sucirta; p. 93, top: © AJ Hackett; p. 93, bottom: © Andi Sucirta; p. 95, top: © Andi Sucirta; p. 95, bottom: © Andi Sucirta; p. 97, top: © Andi Sucirta; p. 97, bottom: © Andi Sucirta; p. 98, top: © Piero Malaer; p. 98, bottom: © Andi Sucirta; p. 99: © Alila Villas Uluwatu; p. 100: © AYANA Resort and Spa; p. 105: © Alila Villas Uluwatu; p. 106: © Amandari; p. 107: © Amandari; p. 108: © AYANA Resort and Spa; p. 109: © Club Med Bali/Accor Hotels; p. 110: © The Laguna Resort & Spa, Nusa Dua, Bali; p. 111, top: © Lee Atkinson; p. 111, bottom: © Novus Bali Villas Resort; p. 112: © Novus Taman Bebek Resort & Spa/World Resorts of Distinction; p.113: © Serene Villas Bali; p. 114, top: © The Watergarden Hotel; p. 114, bottom: © iStockphoto.com / George Clerk; p. 115: © Sarong restaurant; p. 116, top: © Andi Sucirta; p. 116, top: © Andi Sucirta; p. 123: © Lee Atkinson; p. 124, top: © Lee Atkinson; p. 124, bottom: © Bumbu Bali; p. 125: © Café Lotus; p. 126: © Kerin Burford from Kerin Burford Photography Adelaide; p. 127: © Charming Restaurant; p. 128: © Kori Restaurant & Bar; p. 129: © Andi Sucirta; p. 130: © Andi Sucirta; p. 131: © Lee Atkinson; p. 132, top: © Mozaic Restaurant; p. 132, bottom: © Andi Sucirta; p. 133: © Sarong restaurant; p. 134: © Lee Atkinson; p. 135: © Andi Sucirta; p. 136, top: © Andi Sucirta; p. 136, bottom: © Andi Sucirta; p. 137 © Lee Atkinson; p. 138, top: © Andi Sucirta; p. 138, bottom: © Andi Sucirta; p. 143, top: © Andi Sucirta; p. 143, bottom: © Lee Atkinson; p. 144: © Andi Sucirta; p. 145, top: © Andi Sucirta; p. 145, bottom: © Andi Sucirta; p. 146: © Andi Sucirta; p. 147: © Andi Sucirta; p. 148: © Andi Sucirta; p. 149, top: © Andi Sucirta; p. 149, bottom: © Andi Sucirta; p. 150, top: © Andi Sucirta; p. 150, bottom: © Lee Atkinson; p. 151: © Ku De Ta; p. 152: © The Rock Bar Bali; p. 156: © Andi Sucirta; p. 158, top: © Andi Sucirta; p. 158, bottom: © Andi Sucirta; p. 159, top: © The Rock Bar Bali; p. 159, bottom: © Andi Sucirta; p. 160: © Lee Atkinson; p. 161.

Notes